WITHDRAWN

WITHDRAWN

AFRICA UNBOUND

AFRICA UNBOUND

REFLECTIONS OF AN AFRICAN STATESMAN

by Alex Quaison-Sackey

Foreword by Kwame Nkrumah

FREDERICK A. PRAEGER, *Publishers*
New York · Washington

BOOKS THAT MATTER

Published in the United States of America in 1963
by Frederick A. Praeger, Inc., Publishers
111 Fourth Avenue, New York 3, N.Y.

Third printing, 1965

All rights reserved

© 1963 by Frederick A. Praeger, Inc.

Library of Congress Catalog Card Number: 63–10827

Printed in the United States of America

916
Q1a

Contents

16736

Foreword

by

Osagyefo Dr. Kwame Nkrumah
President of the Republic of Ghana

THE DECADE following the early 1950's may truly be regarded as Africa's decade. Breathtaking and significant changes have taken place on the African continent that were undreamed of twelve or fifteen years earlier. The independence of Ghana in March, 1957, proved to be the beginning of a great avalanche which was soon to sweep before it the "possessions" and "spheres of influence" of the colonial powers. A majority of these so-called possessions have been transformed in our time into sovereign, independent states, and the process of decolonization goes on unabated.

Our next goal is to attain the political unification of the African continent so as to give form and substance to our independence through total disengagement from imperialist and colonialist entanglements.

It is about these changes that are taking place in Africa that Alex Quaison-Sackey writes with such force and clarity in *Africa Unbound*. Coming from a distinguished diplomat who has himself been actively associated with some of the political factors affecting the complicated process of evolution, this book should serve to promote understanding of the forces at work in Africa today. It should also assist in creating a better appraisal of the efforts being made by Africans to complete the liberation of their continent from all forms of imperialism, colonialism, racialism, and neocolonialism. In this way, we may secure the establishment of the personality of the African and the fulfillment of his destiny in an interdependent world.

—KWAME NKRUMAH

Accra
October, 1962

Preface

SINCE MY EARLIEST SCHOOL DAYS in Ghana, when I discovered that I had a natural aptitude for politics, I have remained deeply interested in political science and international affairs. As a matter of fact, I became president of so many students' groups and associations, including a study circle in international affairs at Mfantsipim School, Cape Coast—and later at Achimota College, near Accra—that I was nicknamed the "young statesman" by my friends. At Exeter College, Oxford, where I read "modern greats," I continued my political education by taking an honors degree in philosophy, politics, and economics. In addition to my studies, I took part in the activities of the Oxford Union, and the opportunity of serving as the President of the West African Students Union at Oxford gave me an insight into world affairs and both a practical and a theoretical training that was to prove invaluable in the years to follow.

My interest in both national and international affairs, however, does not necessarily qualify me to write a book on any subject. But I have been emboldened to set down my ideas by the encouragement received from my wife, Elsie, and from Nana Kobina Nketsia, Vice-Chancellor of the University of Ghana and Cultural Adviser to the President of Ghana. Moreover, my own travels in Latin America, Europe, and Africa have served to convince me that in the outside world Africa has been the subject not simply of neglect but of ignorance, misinterpretation, and, indeed, distortion. I therefore felt strongly that I had a moral obligation to express my own African views on Africa. And this book is the result.

In the pages that follow, I have attempted to outline the awakening that has occurred, and will undoubtedly continue to occur, among the peoples of Africa and the world. I have concentrated on the African point of view throughout, for I wished, above all, to correct the image of Africa that prevails in the minds of those non-Africans who still conceive of Africa as a dark continent inhabited solely by savages. I have, therefore, examined some basic concepts that are of importance to Africans—for example, the concept of the so-called "African Personality," a term first used by Osagyefo Dr. Kwame Nkrumah, President of Ghana, at the first Conference of Independent African States. I have discussed the movement toward African independence and unity. I have analyzed the doctrine of positive neutralism and nonalignment, which is the cornerstone of the foreign policy of a number of African states, such as Ghana, Guinea, Mali, the United Arab Republic, Morocco, Ethiopia, Tanganyika, and Sudan. And I have emphasized, in a chapter on Africa and the United Nations, the common front presented by the African states on such matters as colonialism and racial discrimination in Africa. Throughout, my intention has been to trace the emergence of the African Personality from its conception as an ideal to its projection upon the world stage at the United Nations, and I conclude with a number of my own reflections—again, largely from the African point of view—on what has been happening in Africa and what may reasonably be expected to happen in the future.

My contention, in brief, is that Africa unbound means the complete and total freedom of all Africa from colonialism, neocolonialism, imperialism, and racial discrimination. Only when freedom has finally been achieved can Africa speak out boldly with her own voice and project a truly African point of view. Only then can Africa begin to develop her own resources in her own way for the benefit of all. Only then can Africa achieve her own renaissance by building her own institutions against the background of her own traditions. Only then can Africa gain sufficient strength and stability to contribute to the decisions affecting the peace of the world. But if Africa remains partially bound, then she will again be dependent upon this or that European, American, or Asian power—and the African Personality will become distorted and warped.

That Africa will remain bound, however, seems hardly likely, for the Africans themselves have already made notable contributions to their own cause. The first Conference of Independent African States, in April, 1958, and the first All-African People's Conference, in December, 1958—both held in Accra, the capital of Ghana—were two such forward steps toward independence and the recognition of maturity. The policy of positive neutralism and nonalignment, which, in my opinion, must become the cornerstone of the foreign policy of every African state; the espousal of a Pan-African viewpoint by Ghana, which has been endorsed by other African states at the United Nations; and, of course, the progressive accession to independence of thirty-two (as of this moment) African states: all these trends have contributed to a unity of purpose among African states in a new era and have drawn the attention of the world to Africa. For this is an era in which Africa has the spotlight of the world focused upon it and in which the great forces of independence are running strong, sweeping all before them.

Even so, the problems that face the independent African governments are immense. In the first place, Africa is a huge continent of some 11.5 million square miles, inhabited by more than 230 million people of diverse economic, political, and cultural backgrounds. Secondly, it is faced with the enormous tasks of eradicating poverty, disease, and ignorance, all of which are subsumed, in turn, by the greater task, largely ignored by the colonial powers, of bridging the gap of centuries during which Africa remained isolated from the rest of the world. All African governments, therefore, have great obligations toward their peoples to provide proper sanitation, housing, technical skills, hospitals, and schools. They must help to emancipate other territories in Africa that are still under colonial rule. They must wipe out racial discrimination and injustice in Africa and thereby help to restore the human dignity of the African. In doing all this, they will be helping to win the respect of the rest of the world, too, and that is why I feel secure in saying that the policies of all African states, both at home and abroad, can, in the final analysis, be directed only toward the emancipation and the projection of what is called the African Personality.

Yet, because Africa is such a large continent, I, too, must be chary of making generalizations that cannot be applied to particular areas. Too many visitors have already returned from one part of Africa with sweeping conclusions that have no relation to the facts, and I must guard against committing the same mistake. Luckily, a number of people have been of great help to me in questioning either my facts or my conclusions, and I wish to thank them all. I must thank Osagyefo Dr. Kwame Nkrumah for the quotations from his speeches. My thanks also go to Mr. M. F. Dei-Anang for allowing me to quote from his book of poems, *Africa Speaks,* and to other writers for the inspiration I have derived from reading their books, which helped me in the development of my arguments. I owe a great deal to Mr. Kofi Sey, Mr. Ken Dadzie, Mr. Kwamena Bentsi-Enchill, and Mr. Frederick A. Praeger for their comments and criticisms. I am extremely grateful to Mr. Thomas Goethals for his understanding yet searching critical comments, which helped in presenting my case succinctly. I thank Mr. Keith Irvine, who provided reference books and offered concrete suggestions, and to my wife, Elsie, who read the manuscript and made helpful suggestions.

To Miss Verita J. Buckman, my private secretary, who spent
much of her leisure time in typing the manuscript at home, I give
my eternal thanks.

   Finally, let me say that I am solely responsible for the ideas
and conclusions I have set forth in this book. I do not expect
that my arguments or ideas will go unchallenged, but if I succeed in arousing discussion among friends, I shall have achieved
my purpose.

                                            —ALEX QUAISON-SACKEY

New Rochelle, N. Y.
January, 1963

AFRICA UNBOUND

And across the parapet I see the Mother of African Unity and Independence, her body smeared with the blood of her sons and daughters in their struggle to set her free from the shackles of Imperialism.

—KWAME NKRUMAH
(*at the Arena in Accra in July, 1949*)

In the pages of the past,
In the faithless days of long ago,
When vision was short, and knowledge scant,
Men called me "Dark Africa."

Dark Africa?
I, who raised the regal pyramids,
And held the fortunes
Of conqu'ring Caesars
In my tempting grasp?

Dark Africa?
Who nursed the doubtful child
Of civilization
On the wand'ring banks
Of life-giving Nile,
And gave to the teeming nations
Of the West
A Grecian gift!

The dazzling glare of iron and steel
Sometimes obscures non-metal worth;
So when I disdained my pristine
Bows and arrows
And cared not much for iron and steel,
They called me "Dark" in all the world.

But dearer far than cold steel and iron
Is the tranquil art
Of thinking together
And living together.

Dark Africa?
Underneath the clotted roots
Of my kingly whistling palms
I keep a treasure that none can measure.

Dark Africa?
My dawn is here:
Behold, I see
A rich-warm glow in the East,
And my day will soon be here.

—MICHAEL DEI-ANANG
(*Africa Speaks*)

Positive neutralism is the refusal of a nation to lose its personality in a world where assimilation is the objective of every great power.

—MODIBO KEITA
(*President of the Republic of Mali*)

How great is the paradox and how much greater the honor that an award in support of peace and the brotherhood of man should come to one who is a citizen of a country where the brotherhood of man is an illegal doctrine.

—CHIEF ALBERT LUTHULI
(*on the occasion of the award
of the Nobel Peace Prize at Oslo*)

I

The African Independence Movement

TEARS SUDDENLY started to my eyes, but I made no attempt to hide them. It was March 6, 1957; I was attending a reception given by fellow students from the Ivory Coast, Morocco, and Martinique, and we were all celebrating the independence of the new African state of Ghana. We were far from Ghana— or so it seemed to me for that moment I stood by myself, apart, watching the convivialities of the guests and holding the glass of champagne from which, only moments before, I had drunk a toast to Ghana's future. We were in Tours, France, where I was studying French, as a foreign-service officer; but the music, I remember, was "high life," which had originated in Ghana, spread across West Africa, and eventually given birth to the samba and the calypso in the Caribbean. Everybody was in high spirits, but I simply could not let myself go. On the other hand, neither could I restrain the tears.

For me, as for many others, that day in March, 1957, constituted a landmark in the history of Africa: Ghana had been born. For one reason or another, the rest of the world seemed to be nearly as excited as we were about this black country that had become the first in Sub-Saharan Africa to graduate from a purely colonial status into independent nationhood. Superabundant good will was everywhere, and messages of felicitation and best wishes, I learned later, poured into Ghana from every corner of the globe. Nor was I alone in shedding tears on that momentous day; for a film I later saw of the Independence Day celebrations in Ghana caught Dr. Nkrumah himself—the first Prime Minister and later the first President of Ghana—weeping as he announced the fact of independence, at midnight on March 5, 1957, to the mammoth crowds that had gathered to hear him speak at the Polo Grounds in Accra. As he said, "Ghana, our beloved country, is free forever," other people took out their handkerchiefs to wipe their eyes. And since then, friends from other parts of Africa have told me that their experiences were similar to mine on the days their countries achieved independence.

For all of us, then, the air of freedom on that memorable day was not an ordinary air, and yet it is difficult for me to describe it. For myself, I felt that I had suddenly become a different person, that I had broken free from some shell or casing that had been preventing me from growing to full stature. This was somewhat surprising; as an individual, I had not felt in bondage to the colonial regime of Great Britain, although I had often resented the way colonial administrators had thrown their weight around in my own country. In particular, I recall, I had resented the manner in which my own uncle, who was a chief (or traditional ruler), was addressed by young district commissioners (as the administrative officers in the field were called)—patronizingly, rudely on occasion, as if my uncle were not a man of education and ability in his own right.

These commissioners, I should point out, functioned at both the provincial and the district levels; for the Gold Coast, as Ghana was known in colonial days, was divided into five main provinces, and each province subdivided into a number of districts, in order to make administration and control as effective as possible. But the very fact that the commissioners, no matter how efficient they were as administrators, did not—indeed, could not —identify themselves with the aspirations of the indigenous peoples invariably led them to the commission of grave errors. Fur-

thermore, their administration was based on the principle of indirect rule—that is, the administration of the country through
the traditional rulers—and such a system tended to enhance the
prestige and power of the chiefs without taking into consideration the wishes of the governed and the traditions of the land.
In Ghana, for example, a chief had never been permitted to
speak in public, for tradition decreed that no one should bandy
words with him; his thoughts and wishes were expressed through
an intermediary, often a linguist, who had been trained for the
purpose and who, in fact, served as a repository for the history
and traditions of a particular state. And yet, under British colonialism, our chiefs spoke freely in public, carried out the bidding
of British governors instead of the wishes of the people, and
subjected themselves to the rigors of nomination or election to
the Legislative or Executive Council centered at Accra. The
Legislative Council was the law-making body, but it served as
a rubber stamp of the Executive Council, which was headed by
the colonial Governor, consisted mainly of British officers, and
was the actual government of the country.

Under the colonial system, therefore, the power of the chief
in Ghana increased out of all proportion to his traditional role.
As a result, some chiefs, such as my uncle, who had become
members of the Legislative Council during the 1920's and 1930's
—because of their superior education and obvious qualities of
leadership—became more and more divorced from the traditional
sources of their power and came to rely more and more upon
the British Governor at Accra for support. Such was the abuse
of traditional custom, under the colonial regime, that even when
the people exercised their ancient prerogative of "destooling"
(dethroning) a chief they no longer wished to have rule them,
the Governor could, through his provincial and district commissioners, refuse to recognize the destoolment and so maintain
the unpopular chief in office. And reverse situations also occurred
—that is, the Governor would engineer the destoolment of a

chief who was popular with his people. In Nigeria, as a matter of fact, a chief was once whipped by a British district commissioner.

In the so-called pre-European Africa, systems of government were generally compounds of monarchy, oligarchy, and democracy. Such governments were monarchical in the sense that a tribe (or a group of tribes forming a state) was ruled by a chief. The emirates (feudal states) of Northern Nigeria, where highly centralized and authoritarian governments developed under emirs, the traditional rulers, are good examples of one extreme. But in other cases, the chief often ruled with the help of a group of wise elderly men—here the oligarchic element enters—who were heads of various families or clans comprising the tribe or state. Although the chief, in such a system, was nominated by the queen-mother of the ruling family (in most African societies, let me add, women are very powerful, and the chief may be either a woman or a man), he had to be presented publicly and then accepted by the people. Furthermore, the new chief also had to recognize the authority of the people, during the swearing-in ceremony, by solemnly promising to rule in accordance with the traditions of the people and the customs of his ancestors. Therefore, in the best democratic traditions, it was also the people who both put the chief on the stool (the equivalent of the throne) and destooled him when they became dissatisfied, for good reason, with his rule. The system I have just described was, in fact, the one practiced by the Akan peoples of Ghana, and it was highly developed by the Ashantis long before there had been contact with the Europeans.

Thus, despite my apparent sense of freedom under the colonial administration, I felt that something was lacking, that I was not yet fully able to mature, to achieve a synthesis within myself, my country, and my peoples of those ancient African institutions that had stood the test of time and of the more recent colonial institutions that had been superimposed upon them. The fact that my country, as well as the greater part of the African continent, was under the domination of Europeans in whom I could see no intrinsically superior qualities was spiritually devastating. It was particularly devastating, I think, for members of my own generation who had been born in the aftermath of World War I, who had reached manhood at about the time of World War II, and who had received good educations in both African and European universities. Yet, even abroad—or perhaps I should say particularly abroad—we who were students found it humiliating to be considered members of colonial territories. African students in France and Portugal were treated, both socially and intellectually, like all French and Portuguese citizens, largely because the colonial policies of those two countries were based on the doctrine of assimilation. But those of us from British colonial territories had an entirely different kind of experience. We suffered all kinds of humiliation in England, particularly from landladies and landlords, because we were Africans. Although my own student life at Oxford—I studied there from 1949 until 1952—was comparatively sheltered and comfortable compared to that of many African students then in London, I could never completely rid myself of the feeling that I was considered a student from a colonial territory—a colonial, in short. Imagine yourself, if you please, walking in the streets of Oxford after an absorbing tutorial and being confronted by an English lady who asks you, "Which of our possessions do you come from?" I clearly remember that I did not answer that question, but it continued to haunt me, and I rather think the tears I shed at Tours constituted my answer.

On looking back upon the history of Africa, I remain convinced that it was unnecessary for the Europeans to colonize Africa in order, as the argument goes, to introduce the benefits of Western civilization. No one disputes the fact that a society that remains isolated from the outside world tends to become static, but that was hardly Africa's situation at any time in her history. Africa had always had sufficient contact with Europe to enable her to reap the benefits, on her own, that such contact offered. But, unfortunately, the greed and avarice of European adventurers and the apostolic zeal of European missionaries, who erroneously believed that civilization and Christianity were synonymous, perverted and corrupted Africa's relationship with Europe and set the stage for the systematic dismemberment of Africa that began in 1885. In that year, the European powers assembled at the Congress of Berlin arbitrarily decided to divide Africa among themselves, setting up artificial borders and frontiers in complete disregard of the needs and wishes of the African people. The independence of Africa was thereby thwarted, her economic and cultural development immediately stultified; and from then on, the Europeans, instead of establishing normal trade relations based on mutual respect and human dignity, used force, bribery, treachery, and deceit to establish the colonial system that prevailed in Africa for over a century.

It is little wonder, then, that to every African, without exception, the independence of his continent is a burning issue. When Dr. Nkrumah of Ghana said, during the political agitations of 1948, "Seek ye first the political kingdom, and all other things will be added unto it," he meant that without political independence (and the liquidation of colonial rule in Africa), it would be impossible for the Africans themselves to confront their own problems of reconstruction—in particular, the problems of disease, poverty, and ignorance. Only when Africa is completely free can the Africans boldly and maturely undertake the huge problem of bridging the gap of centuries of neglect and exploitation. For Africa, as many people tend to forget, once was free, and the modern movement toward independence is, in reality, a re-emergence into independence, a movement toward both past and future glories at once. But since I have discovered during my travels that few people nowadays seem to be aware of Africa's rich cultural past, I am sure that a brief historical sketch will provide some understanding not only of the struggles for independence that the African peoples have undergone in the past, but of the reasons they are so determined to achieve their goals in the very near future. I shall, of course, concentrate on the historical development of the Gold Coast, since that is my own country and I know it best; but what happened in my own country is similar to what happened in other countries in Africa—only the circumstances, the dates, and the colonial power involved vary.

The first European power to trade with my country was Portugal. By 1469, Portugal had, according to João de Barros, a Portuguese historian and Commander of Elmina Castle (1525–28), "discovered the traffic of gold at the place we now call Elmina," a town on the western coast of Ghana, so named by the Portuguese because of the gold mines discovered in the area. Although the Portuguese had been trading along the Guinea coast for some years, they decided, in 1471, to establish a permanent post by building a castle at Elmina. In that year, the King of Portugal, John II, sent one of his courtiers, Diego de Azambuja, to carry out the task; De Azambuja, according to De Barros, was "a knight of his household, who had already been proved in other affairs of considerable importance and great peril," and, upon his arrival, he requested permission to meet the King of Elmina, Chief Kwamena Ansah, whom the Portuguese called Caramança. De Barros described the meeting as follows:

Caramança came—his legs and arms covered with gold bracelets and rings, a collar round his neck, from which hung some small bells, and in his plaited beard golden bars, which weighed down its untrimmed hairs, so that instead of being twisted it was smooth. To impress his dignity, he walked with very slow and light steps, never turning his face to either side. While he was approaching with this solemnity, Diego de Azambuja remained very quietly on his dais, until, when Caramança was among our people, he went to meet him. Caramança took the hand of Diego de Azambuja, and letting it go again, snapped his fingers, saying, *"Bere, bere,"* which means "peace, peace." This snapping of the fingers is a sign among them of the greatest courtesy that can be offered.*

After this reception, the Portuguese courtier informed the King of Elmina of his mission—that he had been ordered by King John II of Portugal to come "to establish a residence in that land." Chief Kwamena Ansah replied courteously, through an interpreter, asking De Azambuja:

> . . . to be pleased to depart, and to allow the ships to come in the future as they had in the past, so that there would always be peace and concord between them. Friends who met occasionally remained better friends than if they were neighbors, on account of the human heart. . . . He did not speak thus to disobey the commands of the King of Portugal, but for the benefit of peace and the trade he desired to have with those who might come to that port.†

According to still another account of this meeting, the Chief replied to De Azambuja's message from the King of Portugal by requesting that the courtier look at the sea and observe the waves. Then he said, "As the waves come and go, so would I ask the Portuguese to come and go."

The stand taken by the Chief of Elmina might well have been the stand taken by other chiefs and traditional rulers in other parts of Africa. But, in many cases, the African rulers, like Kwamena Ansah, were cajoled, browbeaten, bribed, or deceived into entering into some kind of agreement in return for liquor, ammunition, and other tantalizing European merchandise. In the case of Ghana, the Portuguese succeeded in

---

* João de Barros, *Asia*, translated and edited by G. R. Crane (London: Hakluyt Society, 1937), p. 118.

† *Ibid.*, p. 121.

building their castle at Elmina, and settled with us for seventy years (one result of which is that my own language, Fante, is full of Portuguese words and phrases). They succeeded by recognizing the worth and dignity of the Africans with whom they lived, and since they did not bring their women along with them, they freely married African women.

After the Portuguese came the Dutch, the Danes, the Swedes, the Brandenburgers, and then, in the sixteenth century, the English. All these European nations traded with the Gold Coast in gold, ivory, beads, and, unfortunately, human beings, and they built forts and castles along the coast for trading purposes. The Christiansborg Castle, for example, was the seat of the British Government and the home of the Governor of the Gold Coast from 1862 until 1957. (It is now being renovated for official use on state occasions. Interestingly enough, Queen Elizabeth II of Great Britain stayed in the castle as the guest of the free state of Ghana in 1961.) The Cape Coast and other such forts built between the fifteenth and eighteenth centuries are now being used either as military barracks, police depots, post offices, youth hostels, or museums.

By 1850, then, the English had succeeded in taking over the Danish settlements in Ghana, and by 1872 England had become the dominant European power in this part of West Africa. British domination of the coast of Ghana, however, was not necessarily colonialist or imperialist; until shortly before this time, relations between the Europeans and Africans had been based primarily on commerce. The traders had encouraged many Africans to acquire a European education, and in my country, for example, there were Africans who spoke Portuguese, Dutch, Danish, or English, depending upon which castle they had entered for their schooling. Missionary activities had also begun by the early eighteenth century; this we know from the work of the Reverend Thomas Thompson, who was sent to Ghana in 1752 by the Society for the Propagation of the Gospel. He returned to England in 1756 with three African youths who were to be educated there. Although two of them died, the third, Phillip Quaquoo (Kweku), the son of Chief Kojo of Cape Coast, studied at Oxford, was ordained in the Church of England, and returned to Ghana in 1765 to teach and minister to his people. Another Ghanaian, Amu by name, from Axim, became Professor of Moral Philosophy at Wittenburg Academy in Prussia in 1738, and still another, Prince Sasraku of Anomabu, was known as a poet of distinction in England in 1749.

I mention these three men in order to indicate that even before British colonial rule developed there was free and easy intercourse between African and European. It is important to emphasize this point, for there is a common, widespread, and completely mistaken notion that the Europeans had to subject the peoples of Africa to the evils of colonialism and imperialism in order to bring them the greater benefits of Western education and culture. This is, in essence, what used to be known as "the white man's burden"; it may have eased the white man's conscience so to deceive himself, but it brought only misery and suffering to the black man. Therefore, I say that life would have been happier, progress would have been greater, in Ghana as well as in the rest of Africa, had there been neither colonialism nor imperialism. And that is the fundamental reason why all Africans in this part of Africa never ceased to agitate for self-government and independence—a movement that may be said to have begun as soon as the seemingly benevolent interest of the Europeans revealed itself as the tyranny of colonial rule. It is, I am afraid, one of the tragedies of human nature that the interest some men take in others, whether a completely altruistic interest or an enlightened self-interest, is liable to take the form first of pity, then of coercion, and finally of undisguised tyranny; and nowhere has this corruption been more marked than in Africa (as Joseph Conrad, for example, depicted in *The Heart of Darkness*) during those years of the nineteenth century when the Europeans plundered the continent of its natural and human resources.

It was in 1844 that British colonial rule really—though gradually—began in Ghana, for during that year the chiefs of Fanteland, on the coast, entered into a bond with the British. In return for expanded education and continued trade, they agreed to accept British jurisdiction, and George MacLean, who had been appointed judicial assessor the year before, became the first Governor. He was highly respected by the Africans, but at the time there was no question of the Africans owing allegiance to the British Crown. In 1850, however, the Fante chiefs formed the Legislative Assembly of Native Chiefs upon the Gold Coast, with a program for the development of education, building of roads, and establishment of law and order on the coast. And in 1867, the Fante Confederacy was founded by the chiefs with the express purpose of uniting the coastal chieftains and establishing an independent government.

The confederation had a constitution that provided for the establishment of a Representative Assembly charged with the right of taxation. There were provisions "to erect schoolhouses and establish schools for the education of all children within the confederation . . . to promote agricultural and industrial pursuits and to endeavor to introduce such new plants as may hereafter become sources of profitable commerce to the country . . . to develop and facilitate exploitation of the mineral and other resources of the country . . . that main roads be made, connecting various provinces or districts with one another and with the seacoast . . . and that in each province or district courts be established to be presided over by assessors." The movement for independence became so strong that the British Government, which had taken the administration of the colony seriously (before the 1870's, London was not quite sure whether British rule should be firmly established in the Gold Coast) and regarded the Confederacy as "a dangerous conspiracy," took the high-handed action of imprisoning the officers and exiling King Aggrey of Cape Coast to Sierra Leone. This marked the start of the consolidation of British rule in my country. In 1885, the first African member was nominated to the Gold Coast Legislative Council by the British Governor to give the impression that there was an African voice to be heard on this law-making body, but nominations were arbitrary and did not take into consideration the wishes of the governed.

Then, in 1891, the Aborigines Rights Protection Society, which may be called the first political party in Africa, was formed by the intelligentsia with the support of the chiefs. This was the body that campaigned successfully against the alienation of Ghana's lands by the British Crown. An African delegation sent to London by the Society succeeded in convincing the British Colonial Secretary, Mr. Joseph Chamberlain, not to take such action, since the lands belonged to the people. Its legal brief was prepared by a brilliant Ghanaian lawyer, Casely Hayford (1866–1930), who was to write two books, *Gold Coast Native Institutions** and *Ethiopia Unbound*.† In the latter, he stressed the need to preserve African traditions and culture, and he predicted the rise of Africa (the term Ethiopia was then applied to Africa as a whole) to independence and freedom.

Such, in brief, were the methods the coastal peoples of Ghana used to prevent the British from encroaching upon their political rights during the second half of the nineteenth century. In the forest belt to the north, however, the Ashantis, the traditional rivals of the coastal Fantes, were actively and more successfully resisting the British invader. The Ashantis—like the Fantes, Akims, Akwapims, and Asins—are members of the Akan peoples, the major linguistic group in Ghana; by the middle of the seventeenth century, they had organized a powerful kingdom of their own. In 1824, they defeated a British military expedi-

* London: Sweet and Maxwell, 1903.
† London, 1911.

tion at the Battle of Nsamankow, a town in Ghana, and for the next fifty years they continued to make incursions into south-eastern Ghana—incursions that were repelled by the local in-habitants only with the help of the British, who were thus enabled to gain control of the whole of what is now southern Ghana. So powerful were the Ashantis, as a matter of fact, that it was not until 1900 that the British were able to conquer them, annex their territories, capture the Ashanti Golden Stool, and exile King Prempeh I of the Ashanti Confederacy to the Seychelles—an exile that was not revoked until 1924. (According to Ashanti legend, the Golden Stool descended from the sky during the reign of King Osei Tutu, the founder of the Ashanti nation in the seventeenth century. The stool was supposed to contain the soul of the Ashanti people, and it was the possession of it that inspired Ashantis to perform great deeds. The British learned of the Ashantis' great devotion to the stool, whose ab-sence from their midst, they believed, would cause the doom of the Ashanti nation. That was why the British believed they could subdue the Ashantis once the Golden Stool was captured.) Meanwhile, in 1895, a Fante, George Ekem Fergusson, had, by signing a series of treaties with the chiefs of what is now north-ern Ghana, been instrumental in inducing the Ashantis to accept British rule. Thus the Gold Coast, or Ghana, comprised the south (including the coastal belt), the Ashanti north, and the northern territories.

But agitation for independence continued to be led by the intelligentsia on the coast, whose numbers increased as educa-tion spread. Such was the political consciousness in Ghana at the beginning of the twentieth century that Casely Hayford could write, in 1903:

> The general bulk of the people . . . are, generally speaking, intel-ligent, and take great interest in all political movements around them. This is not to be wondered at since every Gold Coast and Ashanti mother takes pride in educating her sons in the tradi-

tional history of the country. . . . Moreover, they are conscious of their destiny, and they are working steadily toward its attainment. Where so-called stronger and more intelligent races have gone under British rule or protection, losing all they hold dear of liberty and political rights, these people have from the first held tenaciously to their ancient rights, political and otherwise, with the force of a logic which no decent British Cabinet can withstand; and, today, their position is unique in the history of British dependencies and of political conceptions, as far as they relate to so-called subject races.*

Casely Hayford was an ardent nationalist (today, his son Archie is a member of Parliament in Ghana); he became a member of the Legislative Council in 1916 and, in 1920, founded the West African National Congress, which found ardent supporters in men like Isaac T. A. Wallace-Johnson of Sierra Leone and Herbert Macaulay of Nigeria. This support, however, created a diversion, as it were, from national politics to West African nationalism, and although it helped to establish political affinities among leaders in Ghana, Gambia, Sierra Leone, and Nigeria, it was bound to slow down the Ghanaian independence movement. In any event, Hayford and other political leaders were coming up against an increasingly strong counterforce between 1920 and 1938—the traditional rulers. For although there was, by then, a powerful and articulate intelligentsia—composed primarily of lawyers, doctors, and teachers—that could conceivably have wrested independence from the British, the chiefs, led by Nana Sir Ofori Attah I and assisted by my uncle, Nana Ayirebi-Acquah III, had become equally strong. Their Joint Provincial Council of Chiefs, established about 1925 with the active support of Sir Gordon Guggisberg, one of the most adroit British governors of the Gold Coast, had served to separate the chiefs from the educated classes, with whom they had been in league since the formation of the Aborigines Rights Protection

* *Gold Coast Native Institutions,* pp. 79–80.

Society. The chiefs were convinced by the Governor that their powers as leaders of their people would be taken away by ambitious politicians unless they banded together. Henceforth, then, the conflict was to lie between traditional authority, buttressed by colonial rule, and elected authority, represented by politicians like Hayford.

In the same year (1925), the British granted Ghana a modern constitution that was supposed to be the most advanced in colonial Africa. But it did not satisfy the nationalists, partly because the franchise was limited and partly because African representation was less than British representation. The 1925 constitution, called the Guggisberg Constitution, enabled the three municipal towns of Accra, Cape Coast, and Sekondi to elect one representative each to the Legislative Council. Only citizens who occupied houses with a ratable value of £6 were eligible to vote. These three Africans were the only unofficial representatives who were directly elected. The six other Africans were either chiefs or nominees of the Governor. The chiefs elected their own representatives to the Legislative Council, supposedly to guard the people's interests; but, in fact, they invariably did the bidding of the colonial Governor, who controlled the Council through his nominees (both African and European), including mining and commercial representatives. For, under the 1925 constitution, there were fifteen British officials and fourteen unofficial representatives, five of whom were Europeans. The Executive Council comprised five officials who were all white and two unofficial members. These two African members had already been elected members of the Legislative Council, so they were merely appointed by the Governor to the Executive Council.

It was not until 1946 that a new constitution guaranteeing an African-elected majority was granted by Orders in Council of the Parliament of the United Kingdom. There were six official members and six unofficial members nominated by the Governor, three of whom were Africans. Then there were eighteen elected African members, thirteen of whom were chiefs or representatives of chiefs. Once again, this was the first such constitution in British colonial Africa, but it was later described by Justice Aitken Watson, who had come to Ghana from the British court to head a commission of inquiry into the civil disturbances of 1948, as being, in fact, "outmoded at birth" because he believed that the people of the Gold Coast were politically conscious and mature enough to have a self-governing constitution based on a wider franchise. For example, the lack of power of the African members of the Legislative Council to frame government policy and to discuss financial matters without the Governor's fiat was frustrating. And the Governor of the country was still the actual ruler at a time when responsible government by Africans was necessary.

Still, the trend of events, however slow it seemed to us, was indeed promising, and all the Ghanaians who had volunteered to serve with the Allies in World War II returned from East Africa, India, Burma, and other theaters of operations with high hopes for a bright and prosperous future. When the news reached us in 1946 of the independence of India, Burma, Ceylon, and Pakistan, none of us—I was by then an undergraduate at Achimota College—could understand why the Gold Coast should not also become independent, especially since the more enlightened Labour Party then held power in London. In 1947, therefore, Ghanaian nationalists organized the United Gold Coast Convention (UGCC), which took as its slogan "Self-government within the shortest possible time"; and by the beginning of 1948, under the able Secretaryship of Kwame Nkrumah, the UGCC had solidly organized the whole country. The year 1948 was an exciting and critical one indeed. Participating in the struggle for independence, I served as President of the Political Youth Organization in Winneba, where I was born, and there we all pledged ourselves to cooperate with other youth movements in the Gold Coast to agitate against British rule and to support the national movement for independence. But in February, 1948, the first incident occurred: Veterans of World War II who were marching to Christiansborg Castle to present a petition to the Governor, Sir Gerald Creasy, a rather timid gentleman, were halted by the police at the now-famous "crossroads" at Accra. There might well have been some resistance offered by the ex-servicemen, but the police, foolishly and without provocation, began shooting, wounding and killing a number of people, among them Sergeant Adjetey, one of the leaders of the ex-servicemen, now revered as a hero. The news quickly spread through Accra; looting began, and riots flared up throughout the land. The UGCC sent a cable to the Colonial Secretary informing him that British administration in the Gold Coast had broken down and that power must be handed over to the UGCC. The British replied by arresting six leaders of the UGCC and detaining them in prison: Dr. J. B. Danquah, Mr. Ako Adjei, Mr. Akufo Adoo, Mr. Obetsebi Lamptey, Mr. William Ofori Attah (son of Nana Sir Ofori Attah I), and Dr. Kwame Nkrumah (the Secretary).

As a result, the Watson Commission was organized by the British Secretary of State for the Colonies to report on these civil disturbances. Soon thereafter, the six detainees were released from prison, having been ably defended in court by Mr. Dingle Foot, a British barrister and the brother of Sir Hugh Foot (until recently, the U.K. representative on the Trusteeship Council of the United Nations). Justice Watson reported that the 1946 constitution was "outmoded" and that the people of the Gold Coast deserved a responsible form of government. And early in 1948, an all-African Constitutional Committee, under the Chairmanship of the late Justice Henley Coussey, was authorized by the Governor to devise a new constitution for Ghana. The members of the committee, which was extremely conservative in its outlook, recommended a responsible system of government based on a cabinet, an African parliament, and a sprinkling of British public officials and business representatives in parliament. The British Chief Secretary, Financial Secretary, and Attorney General were to be members of the cabinet together with the Governor. The dispute that had taken place between the colonial representatives and the proponents of independence over the establishment of the Coussey Committee was mild compared to the one that arose over the Committee's recommendations. For these led to the formation, in June, 1949, of one of the most powerful and unified political parties in the world—the Convention Peoples Party (CPP), led by Kwame Nkrumah. The youth of Ghana, for the first time, united itself, as I well remember (I had not yet left for my studies at Oxford), to become a militant political force willing to risk everything for independence. Our slogan was "Self-government now." And the CPP won the first country-wide elections ever held in Ghana, in 1951, then again in 1954, and still again in 1956—maintaining leadership during the six years usually referred to as the transitional period between self-governing status and full independence. Thus, under the able guidance of Dr. Kwame Nkrumah, Ghana's independence was assured.

Long before Independence Day, however, there had been a deep conviction among the people of Ghana that the gauntlet had been thrown down and that we were soon going to prove to the world whether or not the black man could manage his own affairs. Those who claimed that we could not were generally Europeans; they were fond of pointing to Liberia in derision, claiming that it was a backward and incompetently administered country, neither more nor less than an appendage to the United States. But those who said and wrote uncharitable things about the Republic of Liberia—John Gunther, for instance, in *Inside Africa*—lost sight of an important fact: Independence and the freedom to manage or mismanage one's own affairs are far more important than the material benefits of life. Liberia and Ethiopia may not be economically as well developed as most European countries, but the very fact that these two countries had an independent existence at all—Liberia since 1847, and Ethiopia probably since the dawn of history—served as an inspiration that never failed to refresh and invigorate those of us who were still struggling for independence. It has long been a conviction of mine, and of many African leaders, that economic and educational limitations should never be a bar to independence, for no peoples can reach their full growth, and so realize themselves, until they are released from the domination of others. It was, in fact, because we in Ghana had always held a strong belief in the dignity of the human personality, of which the African Personality is a part, that as far back as the 1920's we disagreed with the British assessment of us—we were not considered "ripe" for independence—and that more recently we shouted from the rooftops our rallying cry: "We prefer self-government with danger to servitude in tranquillity." Nevertheless, despite the excitement of approaching independence, we remained soberly conscious of a great challenge: Upon Ghana's performance as an independent nation depended the future of the greater part of Africa, still in bondage. Therefore, as soon as Ghana had achieved her independence in 1957, Kwame Nkrumah prophetically stated that "Ghana's independence is meaningless unless it is linked with the total liberation of Africa."

Since March 6, 1957, events in Africa have been swift and compelling. The political developments that changed the Gold Coast into Ghana, transforming a colonial dependency into an independent nation, were also taking place in other British colonies at different periods. Nigeria was soon to be convulsed by Dr. Nnamdi Azikiwe's National Council of Nigeria and the Cameroons (NCNC), which did a great deal to make the people of Nigeria politically conscious. Soon thereafter, the Action Group led by Chief Obafemi Awolowo and the Northern Peoples

Congress (NPC) led by Alhaji Sir Ahmadu Bello (who is considered the *de facto* spiritual head of the Hausa-Fulani states of Northern Nigeria) made it a foregone conclusion that independence could not be withheld from Nigeria once Ghana had gained her freedom. In October, 1960, therefore, the Federation of Nigeria attained nationhood; in 1961, Sierra Leone and Tanganyika became independent states; and in 1962, Uganda followed suit. So significant has been the change undergone by British colonial policy since the end of World War II that it is only a question of time before Great Britain relinquishes her hold on Kenya, Nyasaland, Northern Rhodesia, Southern Rhodesia, Zanzibar, Gambia, and the High Commission Territories of Bechuanaland, Basutoland, and Swaziland.

The movement toward independence, has not, however, been confined only to the British colonies; it has been equally strong in what is generally known as French Africa, and it has, of course, been influenced by events elsewhere in Africa, notably those in Ghana. But the political evolution of the African states under French rule has been different in character from that of other states—and for two good reasons: Because the frontiers of the French-administered territories were contiguous and because the French language served as the lingua franca throughout the territories, the French were able to administer them all, in effect, as a single strategic unit. There were, in fact, two main administrative units: French West Africa, which was composed of Mauritania, Senegal, Guinea, Sudan, Upper Volta, Ivory Coast, Niger, and Dahomey; and French Equatorial Africa, which comprised Gabon, Chad, Ubangi Shari (Central African Republic), and Congo (Brazzaville). In addition, there were the French-administered sections of the former German colonies of Togoland and the Cameroons, first as League of Nations mandates and later as United Nations trust territories. But all constituted the "French family" in Africa and were, in general, treated as a single unit.

Unlike the British colonial territories, where British policy remained fairly consistent regardless of which political party held power in London, the French colonial territories were, in a large measure, subjected to shifts in policies, depending upon which government took office in Paris. Thus, when France herself was ruled by Napoleon II, the French territories in Africa were also autocratically ruled, by decrees issued from Paris. In general, however, French West Africa and French Equatorial Africa were, despite vacillations in policy, rigorously subjected to French law throughout their colonial history, although the French policy of assimilation, which remained consistent, modified the apparent severity somewhat. That policy was important to Africans in French territories, for they were, if educated, treated as French citizens and, under an ingenious policy evolved by the French Government, freely employed in any part of French West Africa or French Equatorial Africa—which went a long way, one might say, toward alleviating any sense of inferiority. Actually, French colonial policy made it nearly impossible for the kind of nationalism that became rampant in British West Africa to emerge, since French-educated Africans bathed freely in French cultural waters, so to speak, and their intellectual leaders often had philosophical and poetic turns of mind. If they indulged in politics, they usually derived their inspiration and ideas from political groups or parties in Paris rather than in their own countries.

Against this background, one can better understand the political activities of men like Félix Houphouet-Boigny, the President of Ivory Coast, certainly a great African statesman and one of the most influential politicians in so-called French Africa. Modibo Keita of Mali, Léopold Sédar Senghor, Gabriel D'Arboussier, and Mamadou Dia, all three of Senegal, the late Premier Boganda of the Central African Republic, and Sékou Touré of Guinea are among other dominant figures on the French-African political scene. But it was Houphouet-Boigny's Rassemblement Democratique Africaine (RDA) that first aroused both

French West Africa and French Equatorial Africa. There is no doubt that the history of the recent movement toward independence in French West Africa must be indissolubly linked with his name.

President Houphouet-Boigny is what might be called a conservative revolutionary, and he has displayed considerable skill and cleverness in ensuring his political survival from October, 1946, when he founded and organized the RDA, to the present time. From my study of French African politics, I am convinced that Houphouet-Boigny significantly influenced, for good or ill, the political struggle in French Africa. He did have two great assets: He came from the Ivory Coast, which is contiguous with Ghana and had a reasonably prosperous economy, and he was well attuned to the political currents of the times. He knew, above all, when to retreat and when to advance, when to let go and when to take charge, for he has always been an astute politician.

It was in 1944 that Houphouet-Boigny, then a coffee planter, first became politically active in the Farmers' Union of the Ivory Coast. Two years later, he founded and became President of the RDA, the first African political party to open branches in every French African territory. Soon he was supported by many politically minded Africans from the whole of French West Africa and French Equatorial Africa, and he claimed that he also had support in metropolitan France as well, including the Communist Party. He had raised what appeared to be the beginnings of a political revolution against French rule; but the French Colonial Office swiftly managed to take the wind out of his mighty revolutionary sails. A shower of political favors and economic schemes descended upon Houphouet-Boigny, and, in fact, the support program enjoyed by Senegal was extended to other parts of French West Africa.

France had always prized Senegal, largely because it contained the strategic port of Dakar. As far back as Napoleon's time, however, political developments on the far-away island of San Domingo, now divided between Haiti and the Dominican Republic, in the Caribbean—especially the rebellion led by Toussaint L'Ouverture in the nineteenth century, one of the greatest black nationalists in colonial history and, according to some, of Ashanti origin—led to the application of the newly won French liberties to Senegal as well as to San Domingo. But when the French continued to expand in Africa, they did not extend those liberties to the inhabitants of the recently conquered territories. As a result, Senegal found itself in a favored position in Africa. When its capital city, Dakar, became the administrative capital of all eight territories in French West Africa, Senegal received the greatest share, whether for administration, education, or economic development; and it was not without significance that the Senegalese dominated the police and military forces throughout all French West Africa. Such special favors influenced Houphouet-Boigny's political plans; there was an opportunity to rally French-speaking African nationalists against the French preserves, but the Africans of many countries who had flocked to the banner of the RDA, hoping to win independence and freedom, were soon to find themselves balked. For the politician who had openly avowed Communism softened his stand, and the only explanation seemed to be that French pressure was at work. Furthermore, he fell sick; he went to France for a cure, and there he remained. But although he abandoned even the semblance of an affiliation with the Communists, he retained the RDA organization, which henceforth followed a policy of increasing cooperation and friendship with France. Paris was a meeting place of French-speaking African nationalists, and so Houphouet-Boigny was able to maneuver even outside Africa. The Ivory Coast immediately began to enjoy the privileges that had previously been allocated only to Senegal—improved facilities for investment, administration, and education. And before long,

Houphouet-Boigny was securely ensconced in Paris with a seat in the French Cabinet.

From 1950 on, then, leadership in the struggle for African independence had to come from other quarters; but the events culminating in Ghana's independence, and the fact of independence itself, did not fail to produce psychological repercussions throughout French-speaking Africa. Houphouet-Boigny and the French tried to play the movement down by arguing, during the transitional period at least, that Ghana could not possibly be free as long as the Queen had a representative there in the person of the Governor-General. After independence, however, Houphouet-Boigny was reduced to claiming that Ghana's independence was meaningless; but when he met Kwame Nkrumah during that same year of 1957 (both men come from the same tribe—the same linguistic group, indeed—in West Africa), it was rumored that Nkrumah had made a bet with Houphouet-Boigny that independence would do more for the people of Ghana in the next ten years than the Ivory Coast's nonindependence. And less than three years later, as a matter of fact, Houphouet-Boigny became convinced that it was at least expedient for the Ivory Coast to achieve its political independence.

Despite the fact that Houphouet-Boigny's ardor for the nationalist cause had somewhat dimmed, the struggle for freedom made great strides in French Africa. In the Maghreb (Arabic for the west), which includes most of the states of North Africa, Tunisia and Morocco had gained their independence in 1956, but the Algerian war was then entering its third year. In French Togoland, now Togo, progress was being made, but in the French-administered trust territory of Cameroun, the French employed high-handed methods, including military repression, to crush what was then the best-organized party in French Africa, the Union of Populations of the Camerouns (UPC). It had become disaffiliated from Houphouet-Boigny's RDA and was on

the verge of leading the peoples of Cameroun to complete independence. Thus, throughout French-speaking Africa, the question "What about us?" became more and more common, more
and more insistent; in Paris, African students had become increasingly restless in attacking Houphouet-Boigny for not going
fast enough; and the French conscience was, of course, being
continually pricked, for France could not let herself be out-
stripped by the British in introducing progressive policies into
Africa. In 1956, therefore, elections were held throughout
French Africa, on the basis of universal suffrage, for the various
national assemblies from which deputies were elected to the
French National Assembly in Paris.

During the next two years, however, the French found themselves obliged to consider further positive action, for African nationalism was distinctly on the move. Their hope of subduing
the National Liberation Front (FLN) in Algeria was rapidly
receding, and they could hardly run the risk of fighting any
more such wars in the tropics. In Africa as a whole, Nkrumah's
clarion-call for freedom fighters, made before the All-African
People's Conference at Accra, in December, 1958, was having its
effects, too. Central Africa, the Congo, South Africa, East Africa,
West Africa—all of Africa was, by then, in political ferment.
And in 1958, General Charles de Gaulle took power in France
and called for a referendum to approve the Constitution for the
Fifth French Republic—a referendum that was to take place not
only in France but also in French Africa. This was the first time
that French Africans were being called upon to pronounce their
approval or otherwise in a referendum for a French constitution.

Although the French territories in Africa were to vote either
Yes or *No* in the referendum, it was hardly likely that any territory, under the eagle-eyes of De Gaulle's proconsuls in Africa,
would have the courage to vote *No*. And when the results became known, in September, 1958, every territory had duly voted
Yes—except one. That single exception was Guinea, on the

western coast of Africa between Senegal and the Ivory Coast; and its leader is still a dynamic young politician, formerly a lieutenant of Houphouet-Boigny (until he became disillusioned), and now President of Guinea—Sékou Touré. Under his leadership, Guinea not only voted *No,* but declared its independence from France on October 2, 1958. De Gaulle's reply was immediate and harsh: He ordered all French civil servants to stop working and to prepare to leave the country. The French destroyed official documents and files, broke up furniture, ripped telephones from the walls, even removed ash trays; but the most vicious act of all was their wanton destruction of the supplies of dried milk sent by the United Nations Children's Fund for the infants of Guinea. But if the French were bent on teaching Guinea a lesson, their attempt was ill-planned and ill-timed. For not only were the Guinean people themselves resourceful and indomitable, but, true to African tradition, Nkrumah and Ghana came to the aid of Guinea with a financial loan that tided them over the worst of the crisis. As a result of this aid, incidentally, France mistakenly accused the United Kingdom of deliberately using Ghana to lure Guinea into the British Commonwealth.

So Guinea not only survived and consolidated its independence, but became a member of the United Nations in 1958 and, joining Ghana, spoke out with the free voice of Africa. The impact upon other Africans was electric. Senghor of Senegal, Tsiranana of Madagascar, Houphouet-Boigny of the Ivory Coast, and several other leaders from French-speaking Africa attended, at different times, the Fourteenth Session of the General Assembly of the United Nations in the autumn of 1959. As members of the French delegation, they saw and heard for themselves both Diallo Telli of Guinea and myself speak out firmly on several issues, including the French nuclear tests in the Sahara, which we opposed. From their reactions, it was evident to me that they would not again return to New York except as leaders of their own independent delegations. In 1959, I had the privilege of acting as host to Léopold Senghor in my house in New Rochelle, N.Y., and we spent a whole day surveying the African situation and discussing, among other matters, such concepts as the African Personality and Negritude. I was assured then that Senegal was going to take definite steps toward achieving political independence.

Soon thereafter, Senegal and Soudan formed the Mali Union and demanded independence from France. But a protracted period of bargaining began, into which other states entered on their own account, and it soon became clear that the French intended to lay down certain conditions before granting independence—agreements of a technical, military, financial, and cultural nature that would, in effect, tie the liberated territories closely to France. The Mali Union was the first to complete these negotiations, soon followed by Madagascar and other states, and the result was that all the French territories gained political independence but unwittingly permitted France to retain a military and economic stranglehold on them.

Meanwhile, however, Houphouet-Boigny, the *doyen* of French African politicians and the champion of French policy in Africa, was watching developments narrowly. Since he had come under increasing attacks not only throughout French-speaking Africa but even in his own Ivory Coast, he decided that the moment had come—independence was, in any case, inevitable—for him to make a dramatic change. Besides, he knew that the French had to act quickly if they wished to prevent the anticolonial influence of Ghana and Guinea from penetrating any deeper into other French territories, for on January 1, 1960, with United Nations blessings, the trust territory of Cameroun, administered by France, had achieved its freedom. Therefore, in June, 1960, Houphouet-Boigny—acting as the spokesman for a *Conseil de l'Entente* that linked Dahomey, Niger, and Upper Volta into a customs union with the Ivory Coast—asked for independence.

This had been expected; what had not been expected, however, was that he would seek independence without first signing the agreements France had set as a precondition. The French were taken aback. Premier Michel Debré of France had to act swiftly; he arranged meetings, and quickly reached an understanding: independence now and without prejudice to the sovereign rights of the territories. Agreements could be signed later.

Such, in brief, were the main events that led to the independence of the territories of French West Africa and French Equatorial Africa. When the General Assembly of the United Nations met at its Fifteenth Session, in September, 1960, the following independent republics that had been French territories until only the month before were admitted to membership in the world organization: Central African Republic, Chad, Republic of Congo, Dahomey, Gabon, Ivory Coast, Niger, Senegal, and Upper Volta. Mauritania, which had become independent in November, 1960, was prevented—by a Soviet veto in the Security Council, in deference to Morocco, which claimed Mauritania as part of its territory—from being admitted to the United Nations; but in September, 1961, after some horse-trading involving Outer Mongolia, Mauritania became a member of the United Nations. The year 1960 was, in fact, an extraordinary one for new African states; not only did the Republics of Cameroun and Malagasy (formerly Madagascar) gain independence, but so did Somalia, Mali, and Togo. In addition, the Congo Republic (Léopoldville), whose problems I shall take up later, was also admitted, as the world knows, to the United Nations. Later, the other Belgian-administered territories, Ruanda and Urundi, gained their independence on July 1, 1962 (as Ruanda and Burundi), and became United Nations members in September, 1962. Finally, of course, 1960 was the year in which Ghana, after three full years of independence, proudly became a republic.

Thus the movement for African independence has been growing from strength to strength, from nation to nation, and today there are thirty-two independent African states. The head of every such state has, moreover, agreed with Nkrumah of Ghana that the independence of his own country is meaningful only within the wider context of a wholly liberated continent, and therefore every African delegate to the United Nations espouses the cause of complete independence for every state in Africa.

Once independence has been attained, however, it becomes the duty of each government to strive to reconstruct its state as quickly as possible. After all, the general revolt against colonialism has been based upon the conviction that only under independence can the Africans themselves order and perfect their own lives, and no African can possibly maintain that independence is an end in itself. In my view, it is imperative that independence become the means by which we organize our African institutions to meet the needs and demands of the twentieth century in which we must live. Our traditional African institutions have not been permitted to grow naturally and to mature; foreign institutions have been grafted onto them, especially in the last century, and the results are not necessarily suited to the conditions of life in Africa. Therefore, we must carefully and painstakingly examine them. If some of our institutions have stood the test of time—the systems of government, for example, which I mentioned earlier—then we can surely use them or blend them with inherited colonial institutions, such as the Westminster model of Parliament that was introduced into former British colonies. If the theocratic state of Ife and the kingdom of Benin (now part of Nigeria), which flourished in the thirteenth and fourteenth centuries A.D., could produce the notable works of art that are now so famous throughout the rest of the world, then we must also look back to our own cultural past for inspiration and guidance. In any case, we must work both quickly and carefully, for Africa is attempting to accomplish in a

II

The African Personality

To MANY PEOPLE, the term "African Personality" is both new and strange. Although it has had a long history in Africa, it has come into constant use only within recent years; and it has done so, quite clearly, in response to the vast economic, social, and political movements that have been convulsing Africa since the end of World War II. It is, in brief, both a concept and a force; as a concept, it is defined by those very cultural movements in which, as a force, it is embodied. It is a revolutionary philosophical concept—an ideal—and it is best realized in action.

It is, therefore, no accident that the term first appears to have been given its modern connotations by Osagyefo Dr. Kwame Nkrumah, then Prime Minister of Ghana, during the first Conference of Independent African States, held at Accra, in April, 1958. Just before the Conference opened, he said in a broadcast to our nation:

> For too long in our history, Africa has spoken through the voices of others. Now what I have called an African Personality in international affairs will have a chance of making its proper impact and will let the world know it through the voices of Africa's own sons.

Two days later, on April 15, he said in a welcoming address:

> In asserting our African Personality, we shall be free to act in our individual and collective interests at any particular time. We shall

also be able to exert our influence on the side of peace and up-
hold the rights of all peoples to decide for themselves their own
forms of government as well as the rights of all peoples, regardless
of race, color, or creed, to lead their own lives in freedom and
without fear.

Then, at the conclusion of the Conference, on April 22, he made
another reference to the subject:

> Our earnest and passionate desire is to exert through our African
> Personality whatever influence we can bring to bear on the side of
> peace, in the hope of persuading the two main power blocs to
> come together to find a peaceful and permanent solution to their
> outstanding differences within the framework of the Charter of
> the United Nations.

And, finally, the expression was incorporated in the declaration
issued by the Conference. It is worth noting that the declaration
specifically linked the concept of the African Personality not only
to the foreign policy it envisaged for all Africa but also to the
cause of peace:

> We, the African States assembled here in Accra . . . resolve to
> preserve the unity of purpose and action in international affairs
> which we have forged among ourselves in this historical confer-
> ence; to safeguard our hard-won independence, sovereignty, and
> territorial integrity; and to preserve among ourselves the funda-
> mental unity of outlook on foreign policy so that a distinctive Af-
> rican Personality will play its part in cooperation with other peace-
> loving nations to further the cause of peace.

The African Personality, therefore, is, in the largest sense, the
cultural expression of what is common to all peoples whose home
is on the continent of Africa. The fact that the great majority
of these people have black skins is, to be sure, important (as we
shall see in discussing "Negritude" later in this chapter); but of
greater importance is the fact that the African Personality—by

attempting to transcend its specific physical and intellectual environment, yet without pulling up the roots that nourish it—hopes to create, as a force for world peace and unity, a dynamic political creed. Such a creed will express itself through that personality which embraces the qualities of man both as citizen of Africa and as member of the human race. In other words, the concept of the African Personality is extremely active and vital; it is, in fact, an ideal; and like any ideal, it is difficult both to define and to realize, for it is subject to various interpretations. In general, however, it projects a figure of action and thought, of unified power, which displays itself, and thereby defines itself, in action—particularly in political action, as we shall observe in the following chapter; and it is so closely related to other political ideas such as Pan-Africanism, positive action, and nonalignment that it is sometimes difficult to distinguish one from another. But that is simply a measure of the African's dedication: He is completely committed to embodying his political ideas in action in order both to create and to re-create the integral African character.

For it is extremely important to point out, in any attempt at definition, that the African Personaliy is to be defined not only by what it is in the process of becoming, but also by what it was not permitted to become during the century or more of colonial domination, oppression, and exploitation. As Dr. Nkrumah's statements imply, the African Personality is to be construed not as a simple reaction to the colonial past, but as a complex and positive reaction to—indeed, a recreation of—the distant past, too. For in attempting to rid his continent of foreign and colonial domination, the African is attempting nothing less than the ultimate recapture and reassertion of the dignity of the individual—a dignity which the colonial system attempted to reduce and, in some cases, to exterminate altogether. When, for example, Casely Hayford wrote *Ethiopia Unbound,* he did so to draw attention to a personality that had been "bound" and could not realize itself because of the harsh restraints imposed upon it by the European colonial system. He therefore called upon Africans to be themselves, to become themselves, not to imitate the Europeans; he urged them to preserve their African culture, the traditions and customs handed down to them by their ancestors. And that personality struggling to be born then, beginning to realize itself now, was the African Personality. It is, in essence, the same personality that once, before the gigantic incursions of the Europeans, was in full bloom.

Few people today know of the great African empires of Ghana, Mali, and Songhay, of the powerful kingdoms of Ashanti, Ife, and Benin, all of which flourished centuries before the Europeans arrived in Africa. Yet these empires, and the leaders who ruled them, were relegated, by the colonial powers, to the realm of those things best forgotten. After all, the Europeans said to one another, why let the African learn anything of his past; he might glory in it and reject our God-given duty to civilize him. But one of the greatest writers of North Africa, Abdallah ibu Abdel Azis, known as El Bekri, had observed, only a year after William the Conqueror had crossed the English Channel, that the King of Ghana "can put 200,000 warriors in the field, more than 40,000 of them being armed with bow and arrow."* It would indeed be interesting to know what the Normans would have thought of Ghana; in contrast to it, Anglo-Saxon England might easily have seemed a poor and lowly country.

How many people today, Africans included, know of Kanka Musa, the great Emperor of Mali (formerly the Soudan) in 1307? Basil Davidson describes him as follows:

His going through Cairo in 1324, his camel trains and servants and his wives and gifts and arrogant horsemen, all the trappings of a king whose realm would soon comprise a land as large as West-

* Basil Davidson, *The Lost Cities of Africa* (Boston: Little, Brown and Co., 1959) p. 84.

ern Europe, still lingered as familiar gossip in North Africa a hundred years later; for Kanka Musa went with a pleasantly memorable supply of gold as well as pomp and circumstance. . . . When Kanka Musa died in 1352 he left behind him an empire which in the history of purely African states was as remarkable for its size as for its wealth; and which provided a striking example of the capacity of the Negro for political organization.*

Then, too, there was the deservedly famous Mohammed Askia, the King of Songhay, who encouraged advanced studies in Timbuktu (now a city in modern Mali). The historian Leo Africanus, writing in the fifteenth century, stated: "In Timbuktu, there are numerous judges, doctors, and clerics, all receiving good salaries from the king. He pays great respect to men of learning. There is a big demand for books in manuscript, imported from Barbary. More profit is made from the book trade than any other line of business."† Thus Timbuktu, in addition to being a great commercial center, was also a seat of learning; today, any visitor to Mali can be shown around this ancient city by the Mayor, who still keeps the records of the old university.

These, too, are examples of the African Personality in action, and they are part of what the present-day African wishes to rediscover, to re-create, in order to understand who he is, whence he came; and since he knows that no personality can be fully and effectively realized except in the open air of freedom and independence, he wishes not only to obtain these conditions for himself but to recover what his ancestors once had achieved before they finally succumbed, through conquest, bribery, treachery, and bad faith, to European power. Yet he knows, too, as a result of colonial domination, that his struggle to attain a personality, an individuality, and the equality, dignity, and respect that accompany it, is more difficult for him than for peoples of other colors—and largely because the white man has needed to depict

* *Ibid.*, p. 91.
† *Ibid.*, p. 93.

him as, in effect, subhuman in order to justify his own cruelty and rapacity. He knows it because when he appears on the streets of London, New York, Paris, or Moscow, he is referred to not as a Ghanaian, a Nigerian, a Congolese, or a Sudanese, but as a black man, as if he were being denied any personality at all or, at the best, as if he were being allocated one that has to be bad. He knows it, too, because the same distortions and stereotypes appear in literature, particularly the literature of the nineteenth century, when "the white man's burden" provided a justification for the evils of colonialism and exploitation. In short, the African knows that he must emerge not only politically but psychologically as well.

Such, in brief, are some of the reasons the modern African searches to re-create his personality out of the past. For there have been great personalities in the history of Africa, leaders of men and scholars, whose lives were rich in dignity and learning—men like Emperor Kanka Musa of Mali and King Askia of Songhay, already mentioned, and women like Yaa Asantewa, the Queen Mother of Ashanti and the power behind the Ashanti dynasty during her lifetime. (It was Yaa Asantewa who, in 1900, fired the first shot in what is called the Yaa Asantewa War against the British, when the latter were determined to capture the Golden Stool in order to break the Ashantis' will to resist.)

For a student of African history, it becomes particularly ironic that the land of Chakka, Dingaan, and Cetewayo (great Zulu kings between 1820 and 1880) should be under the control of the white-minority government of South Africa, which is attempting to deprive the African of his human rights—indeed, of his humanity—by means of the policy of apartheid, or racial segregation. In South Africa, the black man is compelled by law to work where his white master wishes him to; he must carry passes on his person and account for his every movement; and he suffers discrimination and abuse at every turn. Since he is free neither to worship nor to cultivate himself in the way he wishes, since he constantly endures indignity, disrespect, and inequality, his spirit is inevitably warped or broken. From my own experience, I can tell what sadness this policy produces: After three years of friendship with a white South African at Oxford, I was told by him that he could invite me to his home only if I posed as his shoe-shine boy. The prejudice of white South Africans, their view that the African was made by God to be a hewer of wood and drawer of water, dies hard indeed. And yet it was there, in South Africa, during the 1820's, that Chakka, King of the Zulu nation, distinguished himself as a brilliant military tactician in the wars between white man and African. Later, King Dingaan took up arms to defend his people against the incursions of the Boers; in fact, the Battle of the Bloody River, fought in 1838, is still well known in South Africa, for all South Africans, both whites and blacks, celebrate the anniversary on Dingaan's Day, (although each naturally interprets its true meaning differently). Even if the military might of the Africans was crushed, the significant point for our purposes is that in Dingaan, the African Cortez (as he has come to be called), there was an extraordinarily strong personality and an eminent leader.

In addition to these African leaders of the past who distinguished themselves in both political and military service, and thereby exemplified the African Personality in action, there is at least one other worthy of mention, an educator who distinguished himself in the field of race relations. He is Dr. Kwegyir Aggrey (1875–1927), an Akan from Ghana who is better known to history as Aggrey of Africa, for he spent his life in explaining Africa and the Africans to the outside world. He received his early education in Ghana, went to the United States in 1898, and graduated from Livingston College, North Carolina, where he taught for a number of years before taking both his master's and doctor's degrees at Columbia University, New York. Then he became Vice-Principal at Achimota College (in Ghana), but died soon afterward in New York. Such was his personality that he was had a special contribution to make and that the African Personality had to be realized through greater educational opportunities. On the other hand, he considered the "blackness" of his color important, too, and he found himself in close affinity with black men wherever they were. He once said:

> If I went to heaven, and God said, "Aggrey, I am going to send you back, would you like to go back as a white man?" I should reply, "No, send me back as a black man, yes, completely black." And if God should ask, "Why?" I would reply, "Because I have work to do as a black man that no white man can do. Please send me back as black as you can make me."*

Like Aimé Césaire, Aggrey continued to affirm his blackness as long as he lived.

The African Personality, therefore, has its sources deep in history, but we cannot speak of its modern exponents in any detail without first describing the concept of Negritude, with which the modern African Personality is so closely entwined. Negritude (blackness) is now indissolubly linked with the name of Léopold Senghor, the President of Senegal and a poet in his own right; but the term was originally coined by another poet and political figure, Aimé Césaire (who might be called the political leader of Negritude), in a long poem entitled "Cahier d'un Retour au Pays Natale," which, although first published in 1939, received practically no notice until it was reissued in 1947. In the poem, Césaire wrote about his return to his native land of Martinique, his return to himself, for he had, in returning, learned to accept what he had been trying to escape—himself as a black man.

Negritude, therefore, as it emerged from this intensely personal poem, is both an acceptance and an affirmation of the quality of "blackness." And since it asserts that the black man has a culture which is the synthesis of all cultures—Eastern,

* *Ibid.*, p. 3.

European, indigenous African—it is, essentially, itself a synthesis, or an attempted synthesis, on a cultural plane. It has, nonetheless, a ring of superiority about it, a note of defiance, and a positive approach which have opened veins of considerable richness in the mine of contemporary culture—attested to, for example, by the fact that poets have become political leaders—and suggest how closely related it is to the concept of the African Personality. The argument has even been advanced that Negritude is the product of French intellectualism and that the African Personality is the stepchild of English liberalism; but such arguments are too facile, too flattering to European self-esteem, to reflect more than a small part of the truth. Negritude may indeed draw some of its ideas from French culture, since both Senghor and Césaire were steeped in French intellectual movements, whether Marxist or surrealist; and the concept of the African Personality may well have derived contributory ideas from political theories, both European and American, since Dr. Nkrumah's wide study of political science, for example, ranged from Thomas Paine's *Rights of Man* to Marx's *Das Kapital*. But these borrowings and contributions have been incorporated, at best, into a new pattern of African design, a new consciousness, and a new culture.

This new culture, however, has two points of difference, political and psychological, from that projected by the African Personality. Since Negritude is, as Senghor himself has said, "a true myth," it has no geographical boundaries as such; its boundaries are only those of the lands in which black people dwell—in both the New and the Old Worlds. Negritude, therefore, includes many different areas and climates—Haiti, New York, Guiana, Brazil, or Malagasy—which may not have a great deal more in common with each other than the concept of Negritude. If there is, on the one hand, a strong cultural tie that the concept reinforces, there is, on the other, the consequent diffusion of political power, perhaps even the lack of cohesive political power. The link between culture and politics is, of course, intrinsic; but the geographical diffusion inclines Negritude more toward the province of poetry than of politics. Its partisans would call this dimension mystical, its denigrators vague. But it is difficult to see how a concept which drew its original inspiration from a small island in the French West Indies, however revolutionary it might be, can be as intense, as specific, and as politically applicable as the concept of the African Personality, which was born on African soil and is linked with specific African goals. Although there is almost always a profound connection between the apparent accidental circumstances of an idea's inception and its subsequent development, Negritude has so far shown no tendency to issue into political action. Perhaps it cannot and should not; perhaps that is in the domain of the African Personality. Yet, what Negritude does, it does brilliantly: the psychological gathering together of all black peoples in order to make a moral affirmation of themselves as black peoples who are achieving a profound spiritual understanding, whatever their conditions, wherever their homelands—from Martinique to Mali, from Chicago to Zanzibar—of the bonds of brotherhood. The appeal implicit in the concept of Negritude was intended to reach all places where the black man has found a haven; and it was Aimé Césaire's forlorn hope that from the islands of the sea, from the cities of the plain, from the mountain villages and the lonely farms, the affirmation of the "black personality" and the acceptance of the integrity of being black would soon arise.

Aimé Césaire, in his "Cahier d'un Retour au Pays Natale," describes the sufferings of the black people sold into slavery and depicts the conflicts within him as a black man:

I hear from the hold below the curses of the chained,
The hiccups of the dying, the splash of someone thrown into the sea—
The baying of a woman in labor—the scraping of nails seeking throats—the chuckles of the whip;

The scurrying of vermin across worn-out bodies;
Nothing could provoke us toward any noble desperate adventure.
So be it. So be it.
I am of no nationality foreseen by the Chancelleries.
I defy the craniometer. Homo sum etc.—
Let them serve and betray and die.
So be it. So be it. It was written in the form of their pelvis.
And I, and I,
I who sang the clenched fist.
You should know the extent of my cowardice.

To flee. My heart was full of generous hopes.
To flee—I should arrive lithe and young in this country of mine
and I should say to this land whose mud is flesh of my flesh: "I
wandered for a long time and I am returning to the deserted
foulness of your wounds."
I should come back to this land of mine and say to it:
"Embrace me, without fear—
If all I can do is speak, at least I shall speak for you."
O I am not to be pitied!
I do not ask for alms,
O you men with good consciences who have never
Murdered anyone, never struck evil blows and whose dreams
are not haunted by any ghost.

Who and what are we? Excellent question.
Haters. Builders. Traitors. Voodoos, Voodoos especially.
For we desire all devils
Those of yesterday, those of today,
Those of the iron collar, those of the live,
Those of deprivation, those of escape,
And we are not forgetting those of the slaver.
Ho! Pity! Hyena! long circle about my rottenness, no justice is
done us.
And on the day of execution we know the hymns to sing in prison.

Give me the courage of the martyr
Give me the savage faith of the sorcerer

Give my hands the power to mold
Give my soul the sword's temper
I won't evade. Make my head a prow
and of my self, my heart,
make neither a father nor a brother, nor a son, but the father,
the brother, the son,
not the husband, but the lover of this unique people.
Make me refractory to vanity, but docile to their genius as the
fist to the extended arm.
Make me commissar of their blood
Make me trustee of their resentments
Make me a man of termination
Make me a man of initiation
Make me a man of meditation
But also make me a man of germination
Make me the executioner
This is the time to get one's loins like a valiant man
But so doing, my heart preserve me from all hatred.
Do not make me that man of hate for whom I feel nothing but
hate
For cantoned in this unique race
You know however my love
You know that it is not out of hatred for other races
That I am the toiler of this unique race
What I want is for the universal hunger
For the universal thirst
I call the race to be finally free
To produce out of its closed intimacy
The succulence of fruits
And see the tree of our hands!
It turns for all wounds notched in its trunk
For all the soil works and lures toward the branches
a perfumed precipitousness
But before landing at future orchards
Let me merit those on the tangle of sea
May I keep my heart while awaiting the earth
May I keep over this sterile ocean

which caresses the hand, the promise of armor,
May I keep over this various ocean
The obstinacy of the found course
And its vigor at sea.

As there are hyena-men and leopard-men, I would be
   a jew-man
   a kaffir-man
   a hindu-man from Calcutta
   a man from Harlem who doesn't vote
   the famine-man, the insult-man, the torture-man
One can at any moment seize, beat up, or kill without having to
account to anybody, without having to excuse oneself to anyone
   a jew-man
   a pogrom-man, a little tyke, a bum
But is remorse to be slain,
beautiful as the stupefied face of an English lady at discovering a
Hottentot's skull in her soup? . . .
Whoever would not comprehend me would not comprehend the
roaring of the tiger.

What madness is my dream of a marvelous caper above this
baseness!
Yes, the white men are great warriors,
Hosannah for the master and the castrater of Negroes!
Victory! Victory I tell you; the vanquished are content!
Joyous stench and songs of mud!
By means of an unexpected and beneficent internal revolution
I honor now my loathsome uglinesses.*

Although Negritude and the African Personality are not precisely the same, there is implicit in the former questions that the
latter does not answer: What is to be done politically with the
black minority groups in the outposts of Africa or in other parts
of the world? Are they to continue to progress toward equality

* Random extracts from Césaire's "Cahier d'un Retour au Pays Natale"
(published by *Presence Africaine*).

with the white majority and eventually to become assimilated in the creation of a new race? If so, then what happens to the concept of Negritude? To whom does it then appeal? No final answers can be provided now, of course, partly because both concepts are still in the process of being shaped and defined. But my view is that the people of African descent in the Western Hemisphere must, first and foremost, continue to strive for the equality that cannot be separated from human dignity, and thereby take their places as effective "first-class" citizens in the country in which they live. But during these crucial years of emergence, at least, they must maintain their bonds with Africa in order to link, and so strengthen, both Negritude and the African Personality. For there is an important two-way process involved which can be beneficial not only to the black peoples of the world but to mankind as well: The respect for each will be enhanced as the other becomes fully accepted.

Finally, however, we must conclude that the concept of the African Personality is, paradoxically, more comprehensive in scope because it is more limited geographically. Although Negritude stresses a common conditioning, a common cultural background, and seeks to reconcile Negro culture with Western culture, the African Personality, by confining itself to the African continent, accomplishes all that Negritude seeks and a good deal more. For the African Personality seeks first to find itself before it attempts to seek reconciliation, and it takes action, creative action, in trying to realize the dreams of Negritude, with which, of course, it has nothing but sympathy and understanding, to which it is closely related. Yet the proponents of Negritude are, by and large, "exiles"—which is to say that they have not lived in the home of their ancestors; the proponents of the African Personality are conscious of their ancient roots, and from this sense of tradition they gain their strength, in action, in the struggle toward individual emancipation and national realization.

All of us must, of course, carry our pasts with us, since we are part of all that we have met; and the more we understand about our pasts, the better we understand ourselves. The African is no exception. He is, however, in a somewhat different position, for his personality is emerging at the same time that his national consciousness—indeed, his whole continent—is emerging to play its role among the other nations of the world. Not only individually, then, but nationally and internationally, he must make a distinction between being conscious of his traditions and being tradition-bound, for traditions unsuited to our modern age can become fetters hindering free action. Therefore, Africa must walk a narrow line in her growth and development: On the one hand, she must draw strength, wisdom, and a sense of stability from the past; on the other, she must make sure that she does not become immobilized or imprisoned by an exaggerated respect for the traditions of the past. Has she not with infinite pain and effort just burst from the prison of colonial control? It would indeed be ironic and senseless for her suddenly to find herself incarcerated in an even stronger prison of her own devising; but no one is more aware of the danger than those who are attempting, largely by political action, to give direction and meaning to the concept of the African Personality.

It is important to remember that the African Personality is a revolutionary concept. People and nations are both propelled to action, as we know, by an ideology or a faith; sometimes, however, they are propelled by a negative force, and they revolt. In Africa, the long history of concentrated colonial oppression could only dam up—rather than extinguish—that force, and it eventually erupted, like a long-smoldering volcano, against the very system that had nourished it. So strong was it, in fact, that it will always be sufficient in the future to whip up intense national feelings against foreign intrusion or domination. Indeed, African nationalists have always regarded colonialism as an evil that must, if necessary, be excised by the most brutal surgery. The invocation of the African Personality, therefore, was intended, in the long run, to help the African realize himself. But its immediate practical aim was to sustain the African nationalist in the struggle against colonialism and then, at the proper time, to help him revolt—to revolt, first of all, against the feelings that had been inculcated in him that his own institutions, his own culture, and even his own personality were inferior, and, secondly, that it was "civilized" to accept alternatives introduced by the colonial rulers, including British officials as well, and by some missionaries.

I have deliberately said "some missionaries" because I refuse to judge all missionaries by the failings of some. Nor can I deny that good works entailing a great deal of sacrifice were accomplished by men and women of the Christian faith who came from across the seas to labor in various parts of Africa. Some of these missionaries had altruistic motives and sought neither gain nor fame; others returned to Europe, after their experiences in Africa, to pose as martyrs who had suffered under excruciatingly difficult circumstances with the "savages." I do not know, however, where to place Dr. Albert Schweitzer, who is, of course, famous for his selflessness and his self-sacrifice. There is no doubt whatsoever that he has done much good in Gabon, where he opened his little hospital and became known as the "father" of the Africans in that country, for he has saved lives and helped the Africans there in many ways. But does his sacrifice give him the right to regard Africans, as he so obviously does, as little children who must be patronized? Despite his erudition, he has apparently not appreciated how sensitive the Africans are to any slights to their dignity. That African culture differs from Dr. Schweitzer's or anyone else's does not make the Africans inferior, yet that seems to have been the assumption, unconscious or otherwise, on which most Europeans have long operated.

It is strange, indeed, that so many foreigners, including some missionaries, seem never to have understood, or even to have

tried to understand, Africa and its peoples. These were the men
who blindly condemned everything African—religion, music,
medicine, even proper names—although the foundations for a
sound educational and cultural future had been laid both in my
own country and in West Africa generally long before the ad-
vent of colonialism. Dismissing all indigenous beliefs as heathen,
they imported into Africa, on a wholesale basis, European church
music, rituals, vestments, and language. I once observed my
little sister, now a grown woman, beating her breast and shout-
ing, *"Mea culpa, mea culpa"*; when I asked her what she thought
she was doing, she could not even explain the meaning of the
Latin phrase, although she vaguely understood that she was ex-
piating some offense she had committed in the house. And such
was the influence of the Christian missionaries of various de-
nominations that all evidence of African culture was gradually
suppressed or eradicated from living memory. Even our names
were purposely Anglicized, in nineteenth-century Ghana, in order to indicate that the bearers had become Christians and therefore "civilized" as well. My own name, for example, is Sekyi
(pronounced Sechi), but it became Sackey simply because my
great uncle, who had become a Methodist minister before the
turn of the last century, wanted it that way. Quaison, meaning
the son of Kwei, was adopted by my maternal grandfather in
1896 at school to show his scholarship. Thus, Obu, meaning
rock, became Rockson; Kuntu, meaning blanket, became Blank-
son; and Dadzie, meaning steel, became Steele-Dadzie. In other
cases, in many parts of Africa, the African name was dropped
completely, and a European one substituted. In these cases, it
seemed as if one's own individuality were gradually being obliterated or, at least, being overlaid with a quality that was distinctly not African.

Perhaps worse was the deliberate attempt to eradicate or destroy our cultural heritage. Since drumming, for example, was
considered by the church to be a heathen practice, African

Christians were at once cut off from the wellsprings of their own culture—the rhythms of African music and dance. On this matter, however, African intellectuals did take a stand against the European missionaries, and therefore African drumming and music were banned only within churches. African medicine, too, was regarded as inferior; and if you were an African Christian, you were expected to seek help from the doctor at the hospital, not from the African herbalist, who had come to be styled the "witch doctor" or "medicine man." And yet it was the herbalist who throughout the ages had cured our fevers and our diseases. His knowledge of local herbs could have been used in the development of curative medicine in Africa, but instead he was condemned, and no distinction was made between him and the trickster or "juju-man," who preyed on our superstitious beliefs.

To affect European clothes was another mark of civilization; and if you did not eat with a knife and fork, you most certainly remained in a state of savagery. You were expected to say "Sir" to every white man, for every white man in Africa, thanks to the colonial system, had a position of high trust and importance. And in the French- and Portuguese-speaking territories, the African, once educated, ceased to be an African. He became either French or Portuguese—which is to say that, whatever the incidental benefits he may also have gained, he was giving up his particularly African attributes and characteristics. In short, the personality of the African individual was systematically being debased and eventually denied, if not obliterated, by the support missionary activity gave to colonial rule.

It is against all such abuses that the African Personality is, in part, directed. The reverse of it, however, and the more positive side, is that the African Personality is symbolic of the pride that all Africans now take, for example, in wearing their national costumes, in eating with their fingers without shame, in substituting African names for the European Francis,

Jones, or Hamilton, and in inviting their friends, once they have entered the house as guests, to remain for a meal, even though they had not been invited specifically for that purpose. All such customs constitute the African Personality in practice; but if they seem rather minor, perhaps even negative, and concerned not so much with what is uniquely African as with protesting that the African's way of life is not necessarily inferior to that of other peoples, they are but part of a larger social revolution, of a greater search for what is truly African. For example, the class systems of other countries are not African at all; in fact, most African societies were communalistic before foreign domination, and such class systems as existed were based on the system of chiefs and commoners. Even then, there were no real distinctions, for every human being, according to African tradition, was as important as another, whatever his occupation. Therefore, the affirmative side of the African Personality is an educational one, to teach the African people that the class system, as only one example, is non-African and to interest them in uncovering, in rediscovering their own traditions. Once a former territory gains its independence, there can no longer be any excuse for its failure to rediscover its own cultural heritage and to rebuild its own institutions in accordance with the conditions, customs, and traditions of the land. Already, for instance, the ceremony for the opening of Parliament at Accra, Ghana, has been shorn of its Westminster trappings. No trumpets! Instead, we have adopted the traditional ceremony of the chiefs meeting with their elders. Now the horns "wail," and the drums "talk."

Thus, with independence, the colonial mold begins to crack, then falls apart. In its place, African leaders and educators are proposing new rules, establishing a new social framework, in which there will be room for the traditional values, for assimilated values, and for new aspirations. On the one hand, African governments are at pains to establish institutions where research into African culture, history, music, and other disciplines can be undertaken; and already, in such institutions as the Universities of Dakar, Ghana, Ibadan (in Nigeria), and Makerere (in Uganda), the movement to revive Africa's heritage is under way. On the other hand, Africans are glad to send their children abroad—to Moscow, New York, London, Prague—to gain knowledge they do not yet have at home, and they do so in the confident belief that the young people will return to apply their knowledge and adapt it to local conditions. For unless they adapt it, embody it, make it their own, their learning will be of little avail to Africa's future; but if they do, then the African Personality will be able to soar, freed at last of any colonial restrictions.

Inherent in the concept of the African Personality is the conviction that the Africans have a rightful place in the harmony of all nations; that the world will not find its true balance, will not become what it aspires to become until the African affirmation has been made and the countries of Africa assume their rightful places among other nations of the world. This conviction is a deeply positive one; it is the result of the situation in which Europe held the Africans for so long, and it therefore contains the lessons of a long, hard, and oppressive experience. As Thomas Hodgkin has summed it up:

> African nationalists believe that they have probed what are called "Western values" and detected the confusions of thought which the words are intended to conceal. Belief in brotherliness—but not in the field of interracial relations. Belief in reason—with the prevalence of occultism and superstition. Belief in the supreme importance of the individual—with the preparation for wars in which humanity can be annihilated. In this situation it is natural for Africans to feel themselves thrust back upon their own intellectual and moral resources, compelled to look increasingly to Africa rather than to Europe for their foundations.*

* Hodgkin, *Nationalism in Colonial Africa* (New York: New York University Press, 1960), p. 179.

This is, of course, a crucial lesson for a re-emergent people to learn: not only that the former colonial powers are not omnipotent, but, indeed, that they are not omniscient—that they are, in short, fallible or, in another sense, only human. And precisely because there is a tide in the affairs of men now sweeping toward African emancipation, Africans are feverishly and energetically attempting not only to rediscover themselves—to re-create themselves, both individually and nationally—but to lay the foundations for a society attuned to the needs and demands of a totally new age, the age into which the African has, so to speak, simultaneously been born and reached maturity. For this is, indeed, a new age—an age not only of jet planes and nuclear weapons and manned satellites, but of the Organization of American States, the European Economic Community, the British Commonwealth of Nations, the North Atlantic Treaty Organization, the Warsaw Pact, and the United Nations. It is an age in which, as some say, there must be one world or none, unity or destruction, and it is an age that seems, nevertheless, to be fast outstripping man's ability to keep his own inventions from destroying him.

It is, then, little wonder that the African looks askance at the institutions of the West and that, as a result, the African Personality partakes of both a national and a continental character. For whatever Africa's immediate economic and material difficulties, whatever the lag in literacy, education, and health, Africa has, nonetheless, sprung, as it were, full-blown onto the stage of the world. And at the dawn of a new age, it has taken a fresh look at itself and the world. Africa's need for unity, for example, is strong, and it is based on good historical reasons, as well as immediate practical ones; but in looking to other nations, it sees that there, too, at last, the need for unity is also strong, and it sees that the chains of the past—old suspicions, rivalries, fears—make progress toward that unity much more difficult than it may ever be for the Africans to achieve.

For example, the Churchillian dream of a United States of Europe still persists. Even now, the Council of Europe at Strasbourg, the establishment of the European Common Market (in which even the United States is becoming interested), and the recent revolution in French thinking that maintains that the establishment of the European Common Market should lead to a politically united Europe—all are encouraging bits of evidence that the dream is not an empty one. Regional groupings, it seems, are growing throughout the world, but in Africa they are taken for granted as a necessary part of the development of the continent as a whole.

For if, as all nations seem to agree, some kind of unity must be achieved to prevent the destruction of mankind, then Africa, too, must not simply be permitted to take her place as an equal partner, but, indeed, must take an active role in pursuing the unity that comes from harmony and peace. And it can do that only by activating its own latent potentialities—as individuals, as nations, and as groups of nations—for her statesmen have rediscovered, and are applying, an ancient truth: It is only by action that character and personality can be built—and the African Personality, will, by becoming the more African, also become the more human and humanistic.

The task will not be an easy one. African leaders and their governments, however, have a supreme opportunity to create the conditions for great achievements in the cause of world peace by the sons and daughters of Africa. If they can so prove their worth in all fields of human endeavor and demonstrate by their united efforts what heights they can reach, if given the opportunity to do so, they will have made the African Personality felt and respected. For the affirmation of the African Personality, especially by its modern standard-bearers, promises the dawn of a new era of peace in which power may be measured not by the quantities of armaments but by the quality of morality. It is, therefore, for Kwame Nkrumah of Ghana, Nnamdi Azikiwe and

Tafewa Balewa of Nigeria, Sékou Touré of Guinea, Modibo Keita of Mali, Abdel Nasser of Egypt, Jomo Kenyatta of Kenya, Habib Bourguiba of Tunisia, King Hassan of Morocco, William Tubman of Liberia, Félix Houphouet-Boigny of Ivory Coast, Léopold Senghor of Senegal, Julius Nyerere of Tanganyika, Emperor Haile Selassie of Ethiopia, and other leaders to realize the great responsibilities they are carrying on behalf of Africa. Let them, then, put aside personal pride and take up the challenge to achieve the unity of our continent. Let them work hard to create the conditions in which all Africans can best and most effectively contribute to the maintenance of peace. For we should be able to teach the world the importance of racial understanding and human love, and thereby infuse technological civilizations with the warmth of a humanistic culture. For we are the men who have suffered, and this is our supreme moment.

III

African Unity: The Meaning of the Accra Conference

FOR MANY YEARS before the African independence movement gained momentum, the need for a wider union and a deeper communion among African states had been the subject of constant discussion. Interestingly enough, it was a Jamaican of African descent, Henry Sylvester Williams, who first began to promote the idea of Pan-Africanism and then, in 1900, sponsored the First Pan-African Conference, held in London. It was at this conference that another great leader of Pan-Africanism, Mr. William E. B. Du Bois, an American of African descent, made his famous statement: "The problem of the twentieth century is the problem of the color line—the relation of the darker to the lighter races of men in Asia and Africa, in America and the islands of the sea." Thereafter, men of the stature of Casely Hayford of Ghana, Herbert Macaulay of Nigeria, and Isaac Wallace-Johnson of Sierra Leone continued to advocate unity among both Africans and those of African descent; during the 1920's, these three were particularly active in working for West African federation, and had not Houphouet-Boigny's RDA been stripped of its federalist character during the late 1940's, it would have contributed to the work these men had begun years earlier.

It was after World War II, however, that discussion began to give way to action and that the African Personality began to assert itself. It was significant, for example, that, in 1945, the Fifth Pan-African Conference, held in Manchester, England, was attended by many future African leaders: among them, Jomo Kenyatta of Kenya and Kwame Nkrumah of Ghana. In fact, Nkrumah was Joint-Secretary with George Padmore, a Trinidadian of African descent who later played a major role in the movement for African unity. By working closely with Nkrumah in his Pan-Africanist strategy and by his writings like *Pan-Africanism or Communism,* he gave a fillip to the ideas of African unity. Padmore now lies buried at Christiansborg Castle at Accra, once the seat of colonial government—a demonstration of the affection of the people of Ghana for this great man.

The early postwar years were exciting days in England, I well remember; for African students, impelled by the new spirit pervading the Conference and its delegates, banded together to talk politics and present petition after petition to the British Colonial Office, demanding the right of Africans to rule themselves. The feeling of solidarity among Africans in the United Kingdom has always been strong; at every university, in fact, there was some kind of African union, and the West African Students Union, which actually embraced all African students in England, had its headquarters in London. I was Secretary and later President of the West African Students Union at Oxford during 1951–52, and I remember that the East African students, of whom there were few at the time, were given strict orders by the Colonial Office (the students were on government scholarships, of course) not to associate with West Africans, especially those of us from the Gold Coast, because we were agitators. But, like our "fathers" before us, we discussed African independence and African unity all the time, for we were resolved to bring about a West African federation when we returned to our homes.

For nearly half a century, then, these efforts had been made—against nearly insurmountable difficulties. For ever since 1885, when the European nations had divided up Africa at the Congress of Berlin, the colonial powers had been in full control; except for Egypt, Ethiopia, and Liberia, there were no independent states in Africa south of the Sahara until Ghana achieved her freedom in 1957. Therefore, it was to be expected that no matter how hard African nationalist leaders tried, it would be extremely difficult to coordinate nationalist policies and impossible to effect any kind of unity, since the mere act of crossing from one territory to another, even to visit one's own relatives, was subject to all kinds of restrictions. For in their eagerness to divide up Africa in 1885, and to divide it so that no single nation would thereby disturb the balance of power in Europe, the Europeans had carved out, from any point of view, completely artificial boundaries. From the African point of view, their artificiality was cruel because the boundaries utterly disregarded one of the most elemental and vital of human needs, ethnic groupings. Peoples of the same linguistic group, and even of the same tribe, were arbitrarily and irrevocably separated from one another.

Let me quickly give some examples of this policy. There are today Africans in Mauritania who have ethnic relationships with their brothers across the border in Senegal. There are Africans in Senegal who have the same backgrounds as those in Gambia, which is, in effect, an enclave within Senegal. There are Africans in Sierra Leone who belong to the same ethnic group as those in the neighboring nations of Liberia and Guinea. There are Africans in northern Ivory Coast, Upper Volta, northern Ghana, northern Togo, and northern Dahomey—that is, in five independent nations—who belong to the same ethnic group. The Sanwis of eastern Ivory Coast and western Ghana are the same people, and there are Africans in both countries who are called Apollonians. The Ewes of Ghana and Togo are the same, and so are the Ibos of eastern Nigeria and southern Cameroun.

Finally, as an example from widely separated areas, there are Fulanis in Guinea and Fulanis in northern Nigeria.

Against this background—and I could go on giving examples to show how unfortunate and unwise the imperialist divisions were—it is easy to understand, I think, my own feelings about African unity. Since the African farmer used to cultivate land freely, moving from one area to another as necessity required, he finds boundaries and barriers an utterly foreign conception. In the past, of course, there were occasional tribal clashes as a result of such free movements; but squabbles are not uncommon among brothers, and surely freedom of movement is preferable to the rigid restrictions and illogical demarcations introduced under colonialism. Yet the question today, for Africans, is what to do about the divisions made by the colonialists and perpetuated, of course, even as former territories become independent nations. The answer is simple: Let every African state become an independent nation and, at the same time, place the responsibility upon the new national leaders to find the ways and means of achieving economic and political unity among all African states. Since a social and cultural unity may be said to exist now, and is increasing in strength, the task should not be as formidable as it may at first appear.

It was precisely for reasons such as these that Dr. Kwame Nkrumah proclaimed in 1957 that Ghana's independence would be meaningful only within the larger context of liberation and independence for all the peoples of Africa. This was the first time that a leader of an independent African state had made such a pronouncement, and it was soon to manifest itself in action. For the idea of an African conference had been taking shape in Nkrumah's mind since he had attended, in 1945, the last Pan-African Conference to be held outside Africa, and he was magnanimous enough to share it with the other African leaders who participated in the independence celebrations of Ghana. By April 17, 1957, only a little more than a month after

Ghana's independence, he had written to all the heads of governments of the independent states of Africa to reiterate his desire to convene a conference of those independent states in order to discuss matters of mutual concern. And since the press immediately publicized the news of an impending conference, the attention of the whole world seemed to center upon Ghana. After all, it was the first black country to gain its freedom from colonial rule, and even before that Nkrumah's dynamism had kept colonial rulers on edge for over ten years. Therefore, there was a good deal of speculation, in the Western world particularly, about Ghana's future intentions, and the idea of such a conference seemed to strike many Westerners as revolutionary. Predictions of failure were as common as predictions of success, and there followed the inevitable guessing games as to which countries would, or would not, be invited to send representatives or delegates.

But Kwame Nkrumah knew what he was doing. He was aware, most of all, of the need to plan carefully for the success of the conference. For if the conference did not succeed, if the heads of the seven other independent states—Egypt, Ethiopia, Liberia, Libya, Morocco, Sudan, and Tunisia—did not reach substantial agreement, then the hope of achieving unity in Africa would suffer a severe setback. Therefore, when Nkrumah visited London in June, 1957, to attend the Conference of Commonwealth Prime Ministers, he requested his friends Ambassador Ato Emmanuel Abraham of Ethiopia and Ambassador Awad Satti of Sudan to help prepare for the new conference. And since all the independent African nations had ambassadors in London —all, that is, except Egypt, which had broken diplomatic relations with the United Kingdom over the Suez affair, but whose affairs were being looked after by the Indian High Commissioner's Office in London—it was, of course, convenient to start preparations there. Even so, some quick work had to be done by the Ghana High Commissioner's Office, as I well remember.

For I was then Second Secretary at the Ghana office, had just received my instructions to act as liaison officer to the various African embassies, and was therefore embarking on my first major job as a diplomat—a job I took especially seriously, let me add, because I instinctively felt that my Prime Minister had his heart in this great venture.

Arrangements for the preparatory meetings were soon made, and on August 15, 1957, at the Embassy of Sudan, the African representatives in London sat down together to talk about Africa and her future. Those present at this historic meeting were: Ambassador Satti of Sudan; Ambassador Abraham of Ethiopia; Ambassador Clarence Lorenzo Simpson of Liberia; Mr. J. E. Jantuah, then Acting High Commissioner, later to become Ghana Ambassador to France and then to Brazil; Mr. Gibril Shallouf, the Chargé d'Affaires of Libya; Mr. Mohammed Essaafi, the Chargé d'Affaires of Tunisia, who was acting for my dear friend Ambassador Taieb Slim; and Mr. Mohammed Saadani, the Chargé d'Affaires of Morocco. In addition, Mr. M. O. Shendi, then Third Secretary of the Sudan Embassy, Mr. H. M. Hassan, then First Secretary of the Sudan Embassy, and I were present as secretaries for this first meeting, and Mr. Hassan and I were later chosen by the participants to act as joint secretaries for the remainder of the series of meetings.

It was certainly an exciting experience to be a part, however small, of such a meeting, and the excitement arose, I soon realized, from watching a group of Africans sitting in conclave for the first time to discuss Africa and African problems. There was cordiality and good will all around; I could see it on the faces of all the representatives during the opening exchange of civilities. Then Mr. Jantuah was asked to explain to the group precisely what the Ghana Government hoped to attain by calling for such a conference. He replied that in calling for this first Conference of Independent African States, Ghana intended not to form either an ideological or a political bloc, but to help the delegates to know one another, establish good relations, and, above all, exchange ideas about economic, political, and cultural matters of interest to Africa and her peoples. He concluded by reiterating Dr. Nkrumah's wish that the conference should be looked upon as a joint effort by all the independent states of Africa and not a single effort by one nation.

This led, I must confess, to the only discordant note of the conference; for to everyone's surprise, Ambassador Simpson of Liberia asked his colleagues whether Dr. Nkrumah had consulted other heads of government before he called for the conference. I, for one, became apprehensive because, as a result of contacting all the African embassies in London, I had received the impression that all the ambassadors had been informed of the proposed conference, that otherwise they could not have agreed, presumably on instructions from their respective governments, to hold a series of meetings to plan for the conference itself. My anxiety subsided, however, when Ethiopian Ambassador Abraham, a wise and calm man, replied that although the idea of such a conference had originated with Nkrumah, the conference itself would belong to, and should benefit, all Africa—which was reason enough, he thought, for all African states to adopt the conference as their own and help to make it a success. His explanation satisfied everybody, and it was supplemented, in fact, by Mr. Jantuah's reading from Dr. Nkrumah's letter of April 17 an excerpt indicating that all African heads of government had indeed been consulted about the conference beforehand.

From then on, there were no difficulties whatsoever; after six meetings, the agenda was prepared, April 15, 1958, was selected as the date for the conference, and Accra, capital of Ghana, was chosen as the place. The agenda makes interesting reading now, I think, partly because subsequent conferences have all kept to the general theme of African affairs envisaged by the first conference at Accra and partly because the individual items will probably continue to form the basis for any real agreement on African unity:

1. An exchange of views on foreign policy, especially in relation to the African continent, including the following:
   a. The future of dependent territories in Africa.
   b. The Algerian problem.
   c. The racial problem.
   d. Steps to be taken to safeguard the independence and sovereignty of the independent African states.
2. An examination of the ways and means by which economic cooperation among the African states might be promoted, based on the exchange of technical, scientific, and educational information, with special attention to industrial planning and agricultural development.
3. The formulation of concrete proposals for the cultural exchange of visiting missions among the various countries, both governmental and nongovernmental, in order to encourage firsthand knowledge of one country by another and a cultural appreciation of one another's heritage.
4. A consideration of the problem of international peace in conformity with the Charter of the United Nations and a reaffirmation of the principles of the Bandung Conference.
5. Foreign subversive activities in Africa.
6. The African Maritime Belt (African states to decide the limits of their territorial waters—whether to accept the 3-mile, 12-mile, 25-mile, or some other limit).
7. The organization of a permanent machinery to continue the work of the conference.

The first Conference of Independent African States, therefore, was held in Accra from April 15 until April 22, 1958, and it was attended by representatives from Ethiopia, Egypt, Ghana, Liberia, Libya, Morocco, the Sudan, and Tunisia—all the African nations independent at that time. In addition, as observers, there were African nationalists from all over the continent, including representatives of the Algerian rebels (as they were then called), led by Mr. Mohammed Yazid, who subsequently became Minister of Information of the Provisional Algerian Government.

Prime Minister Nkrumah, acting as host to the Conference, made a speech just before the official opening, in which he said, among other things:

For months, the ambassadors of those African nations with representatives in London have been meeting to prepare the ground for the Conference, and two missions from Ghana have visited Cairo to consult with the Egyptian Government. Very recently, a delegation headed by the Minister of Justice, Mr. Ako Adjei, visited the capitals of all the other seven participating nations to conclude arrangements for the Conference. Next Tuesday, leaders from all eight nations will inaugurate what I regard as the most significant event in the history of Africa for many centuries. Why is this Conference so important? For the first time, I think, in the history of this great continent, leaders of all the purely African states which play an independent role in international affairs will meet to discuss the problems of our countries and to take the first steps toward working out an African contribution to international peace and good will. For too long in our history, Africa has spoken through the voices of others. Now what I have called an African Personality in international affairs will have a chance of making its proper impact and letting the world know of it through the voices of Africa's own sons. At this Conference, we shall exchange views on political, economic, social, and cultural matters of common concern to all the participating countries, and hope thereby to establish a basis for future cooperation in these fields. We shall not forget our brethren in many parts of Africa who unfortunately do not yet enjoy the freedom we have won. Not only shall we hope to work out means by which freedom so dearly won will be preserved, but we shall also be concerned to give encouragement and hope to all not yet free to decide their destiny. The success of this Conference and the sense of responsibility with which we approach our discussions will, I believe, be a measure of the readiness and ability of all Africans to manage their own domestic and international affairs.

Dr. Nkrumah then went on to say that it was regrettable that the Conference was to be restricted to only eight African states, but he added that the participants had themselves decided that it would be impracticable to invite countries still not yet able to speak for themselves in international affairs. And he concluded: "We regret this omission, which further underlies the urgency of freeing this continent of foreign domination. I sincerely hope, however, that very shortly the opportunity will occur for making the voices of all these other dependent countries in Africa heard."

As the opening date neared, messages of best wishes came in from all parts of the world. From the late John Foster Dulles, then the U. S. Secretary of State, came greetings which assured "the African nations that they can count on the sympathetic interest of the people and government of the United States. The United States will continue to stand ready to support the constructive efforts of the states of Africa to achieve a stable, prosperous community, conscious of its interdependence within the family of nations and dedicated to the principles of the United Nations Charter." Mr. K. Voroshilov, then President of the Presidium of the Supreme Soviet of the U.S.S.R., sent the "best wishes of the peoples of the Soviet Union to the peoples of the African countries, whose leaders are gathered in Accra. In the course of a century the peoples of the great African continent have led a most heroic struggle against the yoke of colonialism, the result of which has been that a series of African countries have obtained their independence. We believe that no forces can check the aspirations of the peoples of Africa toward their independence. I wish the Conference success in resolving the problems facing it, for the good of the peoples of Africa, and in the interest of universal peace." Other messages arrived from

China, Indonesia, Korea, and Vietnam, and from nationalists throughout Africa.

Of particular interest, however, was a message from Dr. Nnamdi Azikiwe, then Prime Minister of Eastern Nigeria, now Governor-General of Nigeria, and one of the ablest political leaders Africa has yet produced:

On behalf of the Government of Eastern Nigeria representing 8 million citizens of African descent, we send our greetings to the Conference of Independent African States now assembled at Accra. Barely seventy-three years ago, a conference of independent European states met in Berlin in order to partition Africa and thereby virtually sentence Africans to political bondage. Your conference is destined not only to act as a unifying force among Africans but also to emancipate them from the thralldom of centuries. The Conference will succeed because it is humanitarian in its aim, libertarian in its objective, and international in its scope. In spite of inspired propaganda to distort the purpose of your Conference, you will succeed in rallying all Africa to the standard of freedom and peace because you do not seek to enslave but to liberate those who are now in political chains, and your purpose is to strengthen those who are free to sustain their freedom. In view of the savage invasion of Egypt and the brutalities now committed in Algeria, and bearing in mind the studied reticence of the African powers and the apparent inability of the United Nations to restrain aggression over weak states, the Conference should consider the possibility of establishing a mutual defense pact among independent African states, in addition to other mutual aids. The problems before the Conference are challenging, but your hearts are pure, your hands are clean, and your conscience is clear. Therefore, as independent African states, you cannot afford to be neutral in anything which affects the destiny of this great continent. We wish you success in your deliberations, and we congratulate our elder brothers from Ethiopia, Liberia, Egypt, Libya, Sudan, Tunisia, Morocco, and Ghana on realizing their manifest destiny in Africa. We regret that Nigeria is politically incapacitated and cannot be represented at this Conference at present, but we fully appreciate the factors responsible. Good luck and divine guidance are our prayers.

Dr. Azikiwe's message, certainly very inspiring, reflected both the hopes and the aspirations of the African nationalists and the value they placed on this historic conference of 1958.

The participating countries approached the conference table with full awareness that not only the whole world but Africa in particular was watching, and they undertook their great task with the confident belief that their discussions would affect for the better the destinies of Africa and world peace. In the fine speeches made at the opening meeting, every spokesman emphasized the need for a speedy and complete end to colonial rule in Africa and the hope of achieving a unity in Africa that would embrace all fields of endeavor. "The realization," said the leader of the Sudanese delegation, ex-Foreign Minister Ahmed Mahgoub, "that our independence and integrity will, forever, be gravely endangered if our economies remain in a state of dependence has prompted us to seek the means for effective economic cooperation among ourselves and to ward off the danger to our very existence."

One of the most eloquent speeches was made by President William V. S. Tubman of Liberia, a man whom I admire immensely for his affability and for his superb efforts to develop Liberia. His praise of the work of others is always generous, as the following indicates:

I pay special tribute to the vision and foresight of Dr. Kwame Nkrumah, Prime Minister of Ghana, for having proposed this Conference, the first of its kind in the history of Africa, for the purpose of providing a forum for the free and unfettered exchange of views on any matters which are of interest to individual African states or to all people of Africa whether independent or not.

And his emphasis upon African unity brought cheers throughout the conference hall:

> Perhaps we should underscore now more than ever the need for unity. In this connection, I am reminded of a story narrated to me by an aged tribal chief at one of my executive councils. He asked, "What is it that causes the death of a snake?" I suggested several answers, which he rejected. Whereupon I asked him to tell me what it was. Instead of answering, he asked me another question: "If a snake came into this room, what would we do?" I replied that we would all get sticks or whatever else we could put our hands on and try to kill it. He nodded approvingly. Then he asked further, "If six or ten snakes came in here, what would we do?" I replied, "We would all run out." And then he said, "That is what causes the death of a snake—walking alone." This story, I think, illustrates quite clearly the importance of unity.

In addition to African problems, the participants discussed the larger problems of world peace, including the prohibition of nuclear and thermonuclear tests, for they were of the opinion that the African Personality must be felt in all the council chambers of the world. "The African," as Ahmed Mahgoub of the Sudan said, "is naturally tolerant—we are prepared to forgive, for ours is not a creed of hatred." And all the delegates agreed that this quality of tolerance should be brought to bear upon the deliberative bodies of the world.

At the conclusion of the Conference, on April 22, 1958, eleven resolutions were unanimously passed, all of which summed up, as it were, the items on the agenda and the views offered by the delegates during the sessions. These resolutions reaffirmed not only the adherence of all African states to the Charter of the United Nations, but the principles of the Bandung Conference, held in Bandung, Indonesia, nearly two years before and attended by all Asian states and six African states (Egypt, Ethiopia, the Gold Coast, Liberia, Libya, and the Sudan). They may be summed up as follows:

1. Respect for the fundamental human rights of all peoples and for the purposes and principles of the Charter of the United Nations.
2. Respect for the sovereignty and territorial integrity of all nations.
3. Recognition of the equality of all races and of the equality of all nations, large or small.
4. Abstention from intervention or interference in the internal affairs of another country.
5. Respect for the right of each nation to defend itself singly or collectively in conformity with the Charter of the United Nations.
6. Abstention from the use of arrangements of collective defense to serve the particular interests of any of the great powers.
7. Abstention by all countries from exerting pressures on other countries.
8. Refraining from acts or threats of aggression or the use of force against the territorial integrity or the political independence of any country.
9. Settlement of all international disputes by peaceful means such as negotiation, conciliation, arbitration, or judicial settlement, as well as other peaceful means of the parties' own choice in conformity with the Charter of the United Nations.
10. Promotion of mutual interests and cooperation.
11. Respect for justice and international obligations.

There were, in addition, other resolutions ranging from such basic issues as the granting of independence to all African dependent territories to the related problems of Algeria, racialism, economic cooperation, cultural exchange, and international peace and security (including such apparently diverse subjects as nuclear testing and the Arab-Israeli dispute). Provisions were also made for April 15 to be observed each year as Africa Freedom Day, for further conferences to be held "at least once every two years," and for a permanent machinery to be established for continued consultation and cooperation among the independent African states. To constitute this group, the delegates appointed their various permanent representatives to the United Nations (the African Group, as it is now called, of which I shall speak in a later chapter).

The implications and meaning of the 1958 Accra Conference were apparent to the participating delegates. Just as the Bandung Conference of 1955 had sent a tremor through the entire Afro-Asian world, so the Accra Conference stirred age-old Africa to its depths by issuing its clarion-call for the re-emergent Africa that had long been dreamed of but had not yet been realized. Throughout Africa, then, nationalists began to intensify their struggles for independence, for they now felt they had the full support of the independent African states behind them. More than ever before, there burgeoned throughout the continent of Africa an awareness, a conviction that the complete liberation of Africa must be achieved so that all Africans could meet together to discuss the ways and means of solving problems common to the entire continent.

The reactions of the heads of delegations reflected this tremendous reawakening, this reassertion of the African Personality. HIH Prince Sahle Selassie, head of the Ethiopian delegation, said: "Africa enters into an era of high hopes and progress, when all Africans, inspired by the Accra Conference, will, we trust, accelerate their march, on the one hand, toward the attainment of freedom and independence and, on the other, toward collaboration, as never before, in the consolidation of independence and progress." The Hon. Charles Sherman of Liberia asserted: "We have now begun to marshal the great latent resources of this mighty continent in the struggle for peace and progress." HE Wahbi El Bonry of Libya said: "We have succeeded, as succeed we must, because our greatest objective was to make sure that liberty, justice, and peace triumph on our continent and in the world." Mr. Mohammed Douri, deputy head of the Moroccan delegation, noted that "our Conference has underlined in a special way the fact that our independence will not be real and complete until the other peoples who are still under colonial rule and who are fighting for their freedom become free." Mohammed Ahmed Mahgoub, from the Repubic of the Sudan, pointed out that "we are all of us striving toward the same goal—a free Africa, a united Africa. And from our unity of purpose we have derived strength for the achievement of our great endeavor." Taieb Slim of Tunisia said, "We have proclaimed the inalienable right of all peoples to self-government and independence and have laid down concrete and practical proposals for achieving this objective." Dr. Mahmoud Fawzi of the United Arab Republic remarked that "the first Conference of Independent African States marks and formally announces the birth of world-minded Africanism, an Africanism which is constructive, broad-visioned, friendly, wide awake, and full of health and vigor." Finally, Dr. Nkrumah, Chairman of this first African Conference, summed up the general feeling by saying: "We have sought not to add to existing world tensions and problems, but rather we have endeavored [to put forth] practical suggestions and concrete proposals which we sincerely believe, if faithfully implemented, may help to bring about just and lasting solutions to pressing international problems which not only plague mankind but threaten the hard-won independence, sovereignty, and territorial integrity of our countries."

That the Accra Conference directly inspired dependent territories to take action was dramatically proved when a ninth member joined the independent states of Africa. For in September, 1958, as already mentioned, France made her unfortunate attempt to punish Guinea for being the sole colonial territory to vote against the establishment of the French Community in

Africa. In the face of this threat to African independence, the Guinean people, under the leadership of President Sékou Touré, displayed both courage and unity, which resulted in a signal victory. Not only did Guinea declare its independence on October 2, 1958, and survive the first difficult months, but the other African states of so-called "French expression" followed Guinea's example. Less than two years later, all the states of the former French Community in Africa had themselves achieved independence; like a resourceful prisoner escaping from a prison, Guinea had made the breach in the wall that enabled the other territories languishing in their colonial cells to follow the way to freedom.

After these first two states, Ghana and Guinea, had achieved independence, not only did the movement toward independence accelerate throughout Africa as a whole, but the theoretical possibilities of African unity discussed at the Accra Conference became practical ones. Since half of the original eight African states meeting at Accra had been countries of North Africa (that is, countries along the Mediterranean seaboard), and since only two of the remaining four (Sudan and Ethiopia) had contiguous frontiers, there had been real difficulties in carrying unity beyond the discussion stages. It had thus been of extreme importance to establish close links between North Africa and Sub-Saharan Africa. As Prime Minister Nkrumah had said at Accra: "Today we are one. If in the past the Sahara divided us, now it unites us. And an injury to one is an injury to all of us." But now that Guinea had attained its independence, it had two independent neighbors—Liberia, with whom it had a contiguous border, and Ghana, a not too distant neighbor—and therefore it became quite feasible to discuss practical steps for achieving unity in West Africa, at least. And so it happened, for the three leaders, Nkrumah, Touré, and Tubman, had similar views on African problems.

Soon after the independence of Guinea, therefore, Sékou

Touré and Kwame Nkrumah began a series of frank and brotherly discussions on Africa, and they agreed upon the need for independence for all African territories, for unity among all African states, and for the social and economic reconstruction of Africa as a whole. The result was that on November 23, 1958, the two leaders signed the Ghana-Guinea Joint Declaration, which begins as follows:

> Inspired by the example of the thirteen American colonies, which on the attainment of their independence constituted themselves into a confederacy, which ultimately developed into the United States of America, inspired also by the tendencies among the peoples of Europe, Asia, and the Middle East to organize in a national manner, and inspired further by the Declaration of the Accra Conference regarding the African Personality.
>
> We the Prime Ministers of Ghana and Guinea, on behalf of our respective governments, and subject to ratification by our respective national assemblies, have agreed to constitute our two states as the nucleus of a Union of West African states.

This joint declaration was followed, on May 1, 1959, by a Joint Ghana-Guinea Declaration, later ratified by the parliaments of both countries. (Later, in 1961, Mali joined the Ghana-Guinea Union. Thus a Minister from Ghana is also a Minister of Mali or Guinea, and a Minister from Guinea is automatically a Minister of Mali or Ghana. Each country has a Resident Minister in the two others, rather than an Ambassador.)

Soon thereafter, Prime Minister Nkrumah and President Sékou Touré met with President Tubman of Liberia in order to discuss methods for strengthening relations among the three nations. A conference took place at Sanniquellie, Liberia, on July 15–18, 1959, in which the three leaders exchanged their views on colonial problems; they discussed racial discrimination, nuclear tests in the Sahara, and other matters, and they agreed that there should be a conference of foreign ministers the following month to discuss Algeria and consider the recognition of the Provisional Government. At Sanniquellie, President Tubman, President Touré, and Prime Minister Nkrumah issued a joint declaration on African unity, the main principles of which are as follows:

1. The name of the organization shall be the Community of Independent African States.

2. Africans, like all other peoples, have the inherent right to independence and self-determination and to decide the form of government under which they wish to live.

3. Each state or federation which is a member of the Community shall maintain its own national identity and constitutional structure. The Community is being formed with a view to achieving unity among independent African states. It is not designed to prejudice the present or future international policies, relations, and obligations of the states involved.

4. Each member of the Community accepts the principle that it shall not interfere in the internal affairs of any other member.

5. a. The acts of states or federations which are members of the Community shall be determined in relation to the essential objectives, which are freedom, independence, unity, the African Personality, as well as the interest of the African peoples.

    b. Each member state or federation shall in its acts or policies do nothing contrary to the spirit and objectives of the Community.

6. a. The general policy of the Community shall be to build a free and prosperous African community for the benefit of its peoples and the peoples of the world in the interest of international peace.

b. This policy shall be based essentially on the maintenance of diplomatic, economic, and cultural relations on the basis of equality and reciprocity with all the states of the world which adopt a position compatible with African interests and African dignity.

c. Its main objective will be to help other African territories subjected to domination with a view to accelerating the end of their nonindependent status.

7. The Community shall set up an economic council, a cultural council, and a scientific and research council.

8. Membership in the Community shall be open to all independent African states and federations, and any nonindependent country of Africa shall have the right to join the Community upon its attainment of independence.

9. The Community shall have a flag and an anthem to be agreed upon at a later date.

10. The Motto of the Community shall be "Independence and unity."

In my opinion, it was unfortunate that the three leaders did not follow up the decisions contained in the Sanniquellie Declaration with concrete action. They had agreed that there should be a conference during 1960 of both the independent states and those about to achieve their independence—including Nigeria, Somalia, and Togo—in order to promote African unity. In any case, the second Conference of Independent African States had already been scheduled for 1960, and it was reasonable to suppose that there the three leaders could implement the Sanniquellie Declaration. But by the time the Conference opened, nearly a year after the declaration, something had gone wrong. The world press, it seemed, had begun to sow seeds of jealousy among the three leaders, as well as among other African leaders, by claiming that Nkrumah of Ghana was attempting to achieve African unity simply because he wanted to dominate the whole continent. And since the other African leaders are no more than human, they were not going to undermine their own positions as political leaders by assenting to a union of states. Therefore, the whole purpose behind the Sanniquellie Declaration slowly lost its force.

Nonetheless, I am convinced that as long as African states continue to meet at conferences, the objectives of African unity should be kept in mind. That is one reason I consider the Conference of African Foreign Ministers held at Monrovia, capital of Liberia, on August 4–8, 1959, as in itself an advancement toward the goals of unity. Although the Conference was designed primarily to discuss the Algerian question, there were, inevitably, other matters to be considered and discussed. In addition, therefore, to a resolution requesting that the Algerian war be ended and that the right of the Algerians to self-determination be guaranteed, there were the following: a request that France desist from using the Sahara to test nuclear and thermonuclear weapons; a condemnation of racial discrimination in Africa; and an urgent plea for the independence of South-West Africa and Nyasaland. The participating countries were Algeria, Ethiopia, Ghana, Guinea, Liberia, Libya, Morocco, Sudan, Tunisia, and the United Arab Republic.

The next major conference was, as I have indicated, the second Conference of Independent African States, which took place at Addis Ababa, Ethiopia, June 15–24, 1960, two years after the Accra Conference. There were fourteen independent (or soon to become independent) states, including the then Provisional Government of Algeria—Cameroun, Ethiopia, Mali, Morocco, Ghana, Guinea, Liberia, Libya, Nigeria, Somalia, Sudan, Tunisia, United Arab Republic—plus observers from nine dependent African territories. Certainly, the move toward independence was accelerating; throughout Africa, as Prime Minister

Harold Macmillan of Great Britain correctly sensed during his visit to the continent in 1960, "the winds of change" were blowing, and more than ten other African states were to gain independence before the end of that year. One of them was to be the Congo (Léopoldville), the date of whose independence had been set for June 30, 1960, by the Belgians.

It is moving, now, to look back upon the Addis Ababa Conference (at which, as at the Monrovia Conference, I had the honor of representing my country as a member of the Ghana delegation), for we did not then realize that our meetings were taking place on the very eve of the fateful crisis of the Congo. There was a general feeling of the imminence of great events because we knew that the Belgian *colons* in the Congo, particularly those in Katanga, and the white settlers in Angola, Central Africa, and South Africa were not favorably disposed toward the approaching independence of the Congo; but the instincts of the delegates were, I think, that a major advance was about to be made toward the goal of African independence and unity. If the Congo became independent and strong, we believed, then Angola and the territories of Central Africa would be emboldened to increase their political agitations for independence. What we did not sense, I see now, was that this advance was to be made through bloodshed and travail rather than through, as we believed and hoped, peaceful and constitutional means. And this we felt despite reports of Rhodesian troop movements along the frontiers of the Congo—which brought the Steering Committee of the Conference together for a whole morning's deliberations. But since the Congo was not yet independent, the committee decided to draw the attention of the Belgian Government to the reports and to ask for assurances that it would counteract such threats. Accordingly, the Chairman of the Conference, Yilma Deressa of Ethiopia, sent the following telegram to the Belgian Minister of Foreign Affairs:

African unity. To all appearances, however, they seemed to progress little beyond the original declaration made at Accra two years earlier; for although the heads of the delegations stressed once again the need for African unity, no concrete decisions were reached. The reason was that the Liberian delegation had asked for, and received, a postponement of any decision on African union until the next conference, at which time a greater number of independent states would be present. In my opinion, the proposal of the Nigerian delegation—that the Conference consider an organization of African states—should have been thoroughly examined in conjunction with the Sanniquellie Declaration issued by the leaders of Ghana, Guinea, and Liberia. As it was, however, a good opportunity slipped by, and the only result, in this area, at least, was a resolution entitled "Promotion of African Unity." It requested the President of the second Conference to address a communication to the heads of the independent states "to initiate consultations through diplomatic channels with a view to promoting African unity," and it further decided to place this item on the next regular session of the Conference, scheduled for Tunisia in 1962 (but which never took place, because of lack of unanimity among the independent African states).

It was rather in economic, technical, and military matters that decisions of far-reaching importance were made. Unity, after all, can seldom be achieved merely by political declarations that stress the virtues of unity, but it can often be achieved by the patient and detailed work of creating channels through which the currents of a growing economic and social life can flow. In this way, like the incoming tide, imperceptibly yet overwhelmingly, African unity will undoubtedly be attained. As the head of the Ghana delegation, Dr. Ako Adjei, then Foreign Minister of Ghana, said, while discussing African unity before the delegates: "The union of African states is the ultimate goal. It does not matter whether you start with an association of African states or whether with economic or cultural cooperation. Certainly, we must start from somewhere, but certainly the union can be achieved in the end."

In short, then, the second Conference of Independent African States accomplished a great deal more than it appeared to do. For just as the Accra Conference had constituted a declaration of intent, and thereby provided a clear signpost for the future, so the Addis Ababa Conference served as a rallying point at a time of crisis, where energies might be gathered and forces consolidated for the great trials that lay ahead.

Perhaps this is not the place or the time to study the causes or the developments of the Congo crisis, which pitted Congolese against Congolese, nearly wrecked the United Nations, and brought the world to the brink of nuclear war. But I must speak of it now, although briefly, in connection with African unity. Ever since the tide of African nationalism had begun to sweep all before it, it had been clear that somewhere, sometime, the forces of colonial reaction would make their stand, and it was in the Congo, during the summer of 1960, that they did so, with all their strength, and, in so doing, delivered a telling blow to the growing strength of a young African nation. With the full support of Belgium, the white administration of Rhodesia, and some financial interests of France and the United Kingdom, mineral-rich Katanga attempted to secede from the new Republic of the Congo. Finally, when Patrice Lumumba, the strong Prime Minister, opposed these powerful forces by trying to keep the republic united, he was murdered in Katanga, early in 1961. Only a week before Lumumba's murder, I had been asked by the American Ambassador to the Congo, in Léopoldville, what I thought would happen in the Congo if Lumumba were not there. He, for his part, was convinced that the Congo would be much more stable, and, as Andrew Tully has pointed out, others evidently thought so, too: "Brutal as it was, however, there was no denying that Lumumba's death had cleared the air and contributed to an atmosphere where steps could be taken toward the unifying of the Congo.* When the United Nations Command finally acted to expel mercenaries and foreign military adventurers from Katanga and to ensure the territorial integrity of the Congo, the United Nations had to fight a war in Katanga not against the Congolese as such but against the mercenaries backed by the gigantic Union Minière and the financial interests of Belgium, Britain, France, and Portugal. Such were the high points in a very confused, often chaotic international situation.

The Congo crisis began in July, 1960, slightly more than a week after the Congo had gained its independence. At first, it took the form of a mutiny within the ranks of the Force Publique, the national army of the Congo. There had been a good deal of dissatisfaction and frustration among the Congolese soldiers because none of them held any senior rank; the army of the newly independent Congo was still to be officered only by Belgians. When the Prime Minister of the Central Government and his cabinet suggested that a new scheme should be drawn up to permit the promotion of able Africans, the Belgian General, Emile Janssen, refused to carry out the orders of the Lumumba Government. He was dismissed and ordered to leave the Congo at once; but when the Force Publique rioted a few days later, it became clear that the mutiny had been engineered by Belgium officers who had continued to tell their African subordinates that, independence or not, the white officers intended to remain in control. Shortly thereafter, on the pretext that Belgium had the right to protect her citizens living in the Congo, Belgian forces intervened from outside the Congo. This was, quite clearly, a direct act of aggression on the part of Belgium and an infringement on the sovereign rights of the Congolese Government. Be-

---

* Tully, *CIA: The Inside Story* (New York: William Morrow and Co., 1962), p. 226.

cause of the Belgian intervention, the Congolese appealed to the United Nations for assistance.

Let me say, however, that Ghana was the first country to which the Congolese Government turned for direct military assistance. But President Nkrumah advised Lumumba to appeal to the Secretary-General of the United Nations for immediate multilateral assistance, and as soon as the Congolese appeal was received, the Security Council met to consider it. On July 14, 1960, the Security Council passed a resolution that authorized the Secretary-General "to take the necessary steps, in consultation with the Government of the Republic of the Congo, to provide the Government with such military assistance as may be necessary until, through the efforts of the Congolese Government with the technical assistance of the United Nations, the national security forces may be able, in the opinion of the Government, to meet their tasks." In the very midst of settling the issue of Belgian intervention, however, Moise Tshombe, Provincial President of Katanga, and Albert Kalonji of South Kasai, encouraged and supported by the Belgians and other European financial interests, attempted to secede from the Congo. Both these areas contain some of the Congo's richest deposits of minerals, especially copper, diamonds, and cobalt and the country's enormous natural resources have always attracted—and, I fear, always will—heavy capitalistic investments in the country by men who cannot readily restrain themselves, for the sake of their own profits, from pitting one leader against another. That was one good reason why Lumumba insisted upon maintaining his strong Central Government to the exclusion of any secessionist or confederalist tendencies and why, when his Central Government was faced with a grave crisis less than a fortnight after independence, he decided to call for a meeting of the foreign ministers of independent African states.

During the last week of August, 1960, therefore, the foreign ministers met at Léopoldville. Although Prime Minister Lumumba had initiated the conference, he had first consulted with a number of African leaders, including President Bourguiba of Tunisia, President Touré of Guinea, President Nkrumah of Ghana, and President Tubman of Liberia. The purpose of the conference, as far as the independent African states were concerned, was to demonstrate African solidarity in support of Lumumba's Central Government and to take a positive stand against Tshombe's attempt, supported by Belgian mercenaries and the Union Minière, to force the secession of Katanga from the Republic. The list of representatives was an impressive one: Algeria, Cameroun, Congo (Brazzaville), Congo (Léopoldville) Ethiopia, Ghana, Guinea, Liberia, Mali, Morocco, Somalia, Togo, Tunisia, and the United Arab Republic.

Since I took part in the drafting of the resolutions, once again as a member of the Ghana delegation, I had a chance to confirm my inner presentiments on this my first visit to Léopoldville that the lack of unity among the Congolese leaders was going to militate against the stability of their republic. The attitude of the Congolese was, indeed, inexplicable. True, urgent business in Stanleyville forced Prime Minister Lumumba to leave us a day after the conference opened, but his representatives were not properly briefed and did not know what they were about. Although Katanga's attempted secession was the main subject of the conference, Mr. Justin Bomboko, the Foreign Minister of the Congo, kept telling the delegates that "Katanga is no problem" and that the Congolese Government would itself deal with Tshombe. But since the Congolese delegation was itself divided on the question of methods, the majority of the delegates at the conference did not feel it should be forced into making a positive stand at that time. I was indeed disappointed, because here was a real opportunity for Africans themselves to mobilize united action; a task force could have been sent at once to Elisabethville to invite Tshombe to Léopoldville and there, in the presence of

African leaders from all parts of the continent, settle the problem of Congolese unity.

At the end, however, the conference adopted four resolutions pledging support and assistance to the Republic of the Congo, and cooperation with the United Nations. Because it reflects the spirit of the conference, I shall quote the main resolution in full:

> The Conference of African States, meeting in special session at Léopoldville from August 25 to August 29, 1960, moved by the spirit of African solidarity and cooperation in the political, economic, and cultural fields, anxious to preserve and strengthen the independences of the African countries which, by their struggle, their sacrifice, and their heroism, have wrested their freedom from the colonialists, conscious of the danger to the African countries represented by maneuvers for domination and division on the part of the colonialists on the African continent, conscious of the need to safeguard the unity of the independent African states and to put an end to all velleities and all attempts at balkanization or secession:
>
> a. Hails the independence and sovereignty of the Republic of the Congo, one and indivisible;
> b. Proclaims the necessity to maintain the unity and territorial integrity of the Republic of the Congo;
> c. Condemns any secession and all colonialist maneuvers aimed at dividing the territory of the Congo;
> d. Reaffirms its full support and backing to the Central Government of the Republic of the Congo, which is the only legitimate and lawful authority, in entrenching and strengthening the independence, unity, and territorial integrity of the Republic of the Congo;
> e. Addresses an urgent and solemn appeal to all leaders of the Republic of the Congo for the preservation of that unity, for understanding, and for cooperation in the higher interest of the Congo and of Africa.

The Léopoldville Conference, in the long run, constituted neither a victory nor a defeat; rather, it was one more pitched battle in the long campaign that is still being waged for African unity. It was held in an African country that was surrounded by hostile colonialist and financial interests—interests that opposed Lumumba because, so they alleged, he had strong leanings toward the Soviet bloc and hence would enable the Russians to gain control over the Congo. The swift unfolding of colonial deception and intrigue, therefore, did much to offset, and indeed to nullify, the immediate effects of the conference, and the later months of 1960 seemed to bear witness to an increasing African disunity on the governmental levels. The enemies of African freedom and unity found a good deal of comfort in the headlines of the press, especially the Western press, which shrieked of open disagreements among African governments at the United Nations, of sporadic or continued fighting in the Congo, and even of the citizens of different African states taking up arms against one another (the clash between Congolese and Tunisians before the Ghana Embassy, Léopoldville, in November, 1960).

It was against such a background that the General Assembly of the United Nations, on September 20, 1960, adopted a resolution to admit the Congo to the United Nations. But because of the continued political difficulties plaguing Lumumba's Central Government, the President of the General Assembly, Mr. Frederick Boland, made the following suggestion:

As members of the Assembly are aware, the situation in the Congo has been the subject of much discussion in the United Nations within recent weeks and even within the past few days, and the constitutional and political position in that country still remains, unhappily, far from clear. In these circumstances, we are faced with a difficulty as regards the implementation of the resolution we just adopted. The difficulty is one for the Assembly itself, and I would suggest to the Assembly that the best solution of this would be to refer it to the Credentials Committee. As I hear no objection to this suggestion, it will be considered as adopted.

Since it was a practical and intelligent suggestion, we agreed to it—both those who favored seating the delegation sent by Patrice Lumumba (as a number of nations, including my own, did) and those who favored seating the delegation sent by Joseph Kasavubu (as several other nations, principally colonial powers, did). By this time, of course, Lumumba, who had originally favored a unified state, and Kasavubu, who had proposed a federation of regions, had split, although they were still serving, respectively, as Prime Minister and President of the Republic of the Congo. Each, on the same day, dismissed the other from his position; immediately afterward, Joseph Mobutu, a young Congolese who had been appointed Chief of Staff of the Congo Army by Lumumba, seized power. He maintained that he was "neutralizing" both posts of President and Prime Minister; he prevented Parliament from meeting and so barred the duly elected representatives of the Congolese people from deliberating. The Congo was now in chaos.

By now it should be clear, I think, that the crisis in the Congo resulted not nearly so much from the inability of the Congolese to rule themselves or to train the required personnel as it did from the aggression of the Belgians and the ineffectiveness, particularly during the early stages of the crisis, of the U.N. officers in implementing the resolutions of the Security Council and the General Assembly. The actions of Colonel Mobutu, for example, the refusal of the U.N. headquarters in Léopoldville to assist Lumumba in flying to Stanleyville to bury his daughter, and the assassination of Lumumba in February, 1961—all these could have been prevented by the United Nations experts in the Congo, I regret to say, if they had been clear about what they were doing. Their work improved, however, and they did a great deal of good in the technical-assistance field, especially toward the end of 1961; but the great lesson for the United Nations is that the effectiveness of its actions lay in the full and faithful implementation of all the resolutions that were passed by the

Security Council and the General Assembly in 1960 and 1961.

In September, 1960, however, chaos reigned in the Congo—so that neither Congolese delegation was seated, and in the light of Mr. Boland's suggestion, it was unnecessary for any nation to sponsor any delegation at all from the Congo and so confuse the situation any further. Yet that was precisely what the United States, under President Dwight Eisenhower, intended to do. In November, 1960, that government invited President Kasavubu to come to New York to present a delegation to the United Nations; moreover, the United States insisted upon a meeting of the Credentials Committee, where it held an automatic majority, and then obtained approval for the list of Congolese delegates submitted by President Kasavubu. Of course, I fought hard in the Assembly against this obvious maneuver. I did so because of strong personal convictions, not simply because of my government's decision to oppose the United States on this issue, and I did so despite a division for the first time among the African delegations. For most of the newly admitted French-speaking delegations from Africa supported the Kasavubu candidacy.

I doubt that the United Nations had ever before heard such bitter debate or witnessed such crass pressure politics as it did during the month of November, 1960—or at least until November 22, when the credentials of the Kasavubu delegation were finally accepted. So strong were the railroading tactics, so furious the charges and countercharges, and so thick the suspicions that all delegations, including the African ones, seemed divided solely along the lines of Cold War allegiances—for or against the United States or Russia. This should not have been so, since it was solely an African issue. Because, for example, Russia supported Ghana's stand on the Congolese issue, ex-Foreign Minister Charles Okala of Cameroun coined the phrase "Quaison-Sackey–Zorin, Incorporated." Appearances, however, were misleading, for the decision by several African nations to support the Kasavubu delegation was the outcome of a conference held in Abidjan, Ivory Coast, in October, 1960. There an attempt had been made to harmonize the policies of the African nations of "French expression," which had, of course, only recently won their independence. It must be remembered, however, as an inescapable economic and political fact, that the budgets of many of these African states had, since independence, been subsidized largely by France—in some cases to the extent of more than 50 per cent of the regular budget, which does not take into consideration the finance capital for economic development. Hence, the surprising fact about many of these nations has been not so much that they have followed policies favorable to France, but rather that they have managed, under the circumstances, to defend African interests as ably as they have.

The division in African ranks caused by the Congo crisis has taken time to heal. And it has, although indirectly, led to the rise of several splinter groups, with the unfortunate effect of retarding the movement toward either an association or a union of African states. I do not, of course, begrudge any number of African states forming a group; but I become uneasy if such a grouping is based on a common allegiance, whether for economic or sentimental reasons, to a former colonial power, for then it becomes difficult either to enlarge the group or to make cooperation with other African states effective. Moreover, colonial powers find a way of returning to Africa in disguise, often by means of economic agreements; and any independent African nation that allows a colonial power to exercise control, however remotely, is retarding our march toward complete freedom and unity. Such neocolonialism must be opposed at all costs.

The first such splinter group was formed by Cameroun, Central African Republic, Chad, Congo (Brazzaville), Dahomey, Gabon, Ivory Coast, Malagasy Republic, Mauritania, Niger, Senegal and Upper Volta. All these states were once under French colonial administration and now maintain strong ties with France. Their heads of state met at Brazzaville on December 15–

19, 1960, for the so-called Brazzaville Conference. (They became known as the Brazzaville Group or the Brazzaville Twelve until, at their third meeting, in 1961, they chose the official name of the Union of African States and Malagasy.) It was, I think, ironic that Brazzaville should have been chosen: For, in 1943, it had served as the rallying point, during General Charles de Gaulle's sojourn there, for the anti-Nazi forces; now, in 1960, it had become the rallying point for pro-colonial forces instead. Although the conference had been called primarily to discuss the tactics to be adopted in regard to Mauritania's admission to the United Nations, the delegates also discussed both the Algerian and Congo situations. On the former question, they paid homage to General de Gaulle, much to the surprise of African national-ists engaged in fighting for their freedom, and disapproved of the idea of a referendum in Algeria under the auspices of the United Nations, which was precisely what the Algerian Provisional Gov-ernment had asked of their supporters at the United Nations. On the Congo, their stand was equivocal; they merely supported President Kasavubu's proposal for a roundtable conference of Congolese leaders that "would group together the representatives of every party without exception"—a proposal that conveniently ignored the fact that there was a duly elected Parliament in the Congo (Léopoldville) which had to be called into being first. On one matter, however, the delegates did make a far-reaching decision: the creation of a commission to study and to propose, with a view to establishing a plan of African and Malagasy eco-nomic cooperation, adequate solutions to such problems as money and credit in their developing countries, the creation of price-stabilization funds, the financing and harmonization of different national economic plans, and the association of these states in the Common Market.

The second splinter group was the so-called Casablanca Group of African states—Algeria, Ghana, Guinea, Libya, Mali, Mo-rocco, and United Arab Republic. The heads of these nations met at Casablanca on January 3–7, 1961, to discuss problems affecting Africa and the world. They adopted an African Charter and passed a number of resolutions, including the following: on Palestine—in which they insisted on the restoration to the Arabs of Palestine of their legitimate rights and made special mention of Israel as being an instrument in the service of neocolonialism and imperialism; on Mauritania—in which they approved of any action taken by Morocco in regard to Mauritania for the restoration of Morocco's legitimate rights; on nuclear testing—in which they opposed the carrying out of nuclear tests by France on the African continent; on apartheid—in which they called upon the United Nations to invoke the sanctions provided for in Articles 40–41 of the United Nations Charter if the Government of the Republic of South Africa did not put an end to its policy of racial discrimination; and on Algeria—in which they declared their determination to support by all means the Algerian people and the Provisional Government of the Algerian Republic in their struggle for the independence of that state.

The delegates also issued a communiqué on the situation in the Congo, and because the issue is still a live one, I shall quote it in full:

[The Conference]
1. Declares the intention and determination of the respective governments represented to withdraw their troops and other military personnel placed under the United Nations Command in the Congo.
2. Reaffirms its recognition of the elected Parliament and legally constituted Government of the Republic of the Congo which came into being on June 30, 1960.
3. Convinced that the only justification for the presence of the United Nations troops in the Congo is:
   a. To answer the appeals of the legitimate Government of the Republic of the Congo at whose request the United Nations decided to create its operational command;

  b. To implement the decisions of the Security Council in respect of the situation in the Congo;

  c. To safeguard the unity and independence of the Republic of the Congo and preserve its territorial integrity;

Urges the United Nations to act immediately to:

  a. Disarm and disband the lawless bands of Mobutu;

  b. Release from prison and detention all members of the Parliament and legitimate Government of the Republic of the Congo;

  c. Reconvene the Parliament of the Republic of the Congo;

  d. Eliminate from the Congo all Belgian and other foreign military and paramilitary personnel not belonging to the United Nations Operational Command whether operating as such or in disguise;

  e. Release to the legitimate Government of the Congo all civil and military airports, radio stations, and other establishments, now unlawfully withheld from that Govment;

  f. Prevent the Belgians from using the United Nations Trust Territory of Ruanda-Urundi as a base to commit aggression, direct or indirect, or to launch armed attacks against the Republic of the Congo.

4. Decides that if the purposes and principles which justified the presence of the United Nations Operational Command in the Republic of the Congo are not realized and respected, then the states here represented reserve the right to take appropriate action.

It is perfectly true that the Casablanca countries have been, as the above indicates, a militant group and that all of them pursue foreign policies of positive neutralism and nonalignment; it is, nevertheless, unfortunate that there should have to be such a splinter group, which came into existence by no such design. If all the heads of state invited by the late King Mohammed V of Morocco had been able to meet at Casablanca early in 1961, the situation might well have been different. As it turned out, however, the Brazzaville Group did not attend because of its support of Mauritania, and other heads of state were unable to attend for other reasons—one of the most compelling being the palace *coup d'état* that detained the Emperor of Ethiopia.

The third splinter group assembled at Monrovia on May 8–12, 1961, for what is generally known as the Monrovia Conference, with the heads of state or government of the following countries in attendance: Cameroun, Chad, Congo (Brazzaville), Dahomey, Ivory Coast, Malagasy Republic, Mauritania, Niger, Nigeria, Senegal, Sierra Leone, Somalia, and Upper Volta. In addition, representatives from the Central African Republic, Ethiopia, Gabon, Libya, and Tunisia were present. The conference also passed resolutions on Algeria, the Congo, Angola, the Republic of South Africa, disarmament, and the United Nations. One resolution, on the means of promoting better understanding and cooperation toward achieving unity in Africa and Malagasy, is worth quoting:

Recognizing the historical importance of the Conference in Monrovia, because of the number of participating states;

Noting with deep regret the absence of some of our sister states;

Confident in their intense desire for African solidarity and expressing the hope that they may find it convenient to attend subsequent meetings;

Anxious to promote henceforth a full and brotherly cooperation between independent African and Malagasy states;

Considering the need for pooling resources and coordinating efforts in order to overcome the barriers of growth which confront all African and Malagasy countries on their way to development:

A. Solemnly affirms and adopts the following principles which shall govern the relationship between the African and Malagasy states:

    1. Absolute equality of African and Malagasy states whatever may be the size of their territories, the density of their populations, or the value of their possessions;

    2. Noninterference in the internal affairs of states;

3. Respect for the sovereignty of each state and its in-alienable right to the existence and development of its personality;

4. Unqualified condemnation of outside subversive action by neighboring states;

5. Promotion of cooperation throughout Africa, based upon tolerance, solidarity, and good-neighbor relations, peri-odical exchange of views, and nonacceptance of any leadership;

6. The unity that is aimed to be achieved at the moment is not the political integration of sovereign African states, but unity of aspirations and of action considered from the point of view of African social solidarity and politi-cal identity;

B. Urges that all African and Malagasy states shall refrain from encouraging, directly or indirectly, dissident groups or indi-viduals of other states in subversive activities by permitting their own states to be used as bases from which dissidents may operate, or by financing dissidents in other countries or other-wise;

C. Accepts in principle that an inter-African and Malagasy ad-visory organization shall be created, the essential purpose of which shall be to put into effect the above-mentioned princi-ples and to establish this organization at the next conference;

D. Decides:

1. That a technical commission of experts designated by the respective states shall be created and that these ex-perts shall meet in Dakar, Senegal, within three months after the close of this conference for the purpose of working out detailed plans for economic and technical cooperation, as well as for communication and trans-portation among African and Malagasy states;

2. That the existing research and technical institutions shall constitute effective machinery for the collection of data and the dissemination of the results of research among African and Malagasy states, and that all states shall so direct;

3. That all African and Malagasy states shall recognize the desire to promote the revival of African culture and traditions in the interest of preserving the real African heritage;

4. That all African and Malagasy states shall make a special effort to include in addition to their respective national and official languages the teaching of the French and English languages;

E. Decides, finally, that the next conference of the heads of African and Malagasy states shall be held in Lagos, Nigeria.

These, then comprise the three major splinter groups in Africa, and I have presented their views to suggest how concerned all three are with the same general problems. That is reason enough, it seems to me—despite the more radical approach the Casablanca Group has adopted, for example, on such questions as Algeria and the Congo—to argue that splinter groups are unnecessary in Africa. Furthermore, the very existence of such groups makes it possible for non-Africans to pin labels on us, to catalogue us, and thereby, whether intentionally or not, cause further divisions among us. Only the utmost dedication to the cause of African unity will surmount such divisive pressures, and I am confident that it will continue to be forthcoming from all Africans. In fact, I had high hopes that the conference held in Lagos during January, 1962, would bring together the various splinter groups; but when the Brazzaville Group objected to the representation of Algeria, it became difficult for the Casablanca Group, of which Algeria is a member, to attend. Yet I firmly believe that African leaders must stop at nothing to advance African unity and eventually bring into being a union of all African states.

There are, as I have said, various ways to do so, and for this reason the establishment of the United Nations Economic Commission for Africa, at Addis Ababa, in 1958, has proved of the greatest significance. Today, as a matter of fact, the United Nations Economic Commission is the only inter-African organization to which *all* the independent African states openly adhere. This, in itself, heralds the political unity to come, for such unity will be greatly aided by the development of telecommunications, aerial links, road transport, and agreements for financial interchanges, to name but a few. The importance of economics in general has been affirmed by several of the African conferences I have mentioned; the second Conference of Independent African States, for example, recommended that an organization to be known as the Council for African Economic Cooperation be established, and future conferences will undoubtedly continue to promote such ideas.

Whenever I travel through the United States, I become even more convinced that we in Africa need to pool our great resources in much the same way. And in an age in which practical men can seriously consider the possibility of the United States joining the European Common Market, it is clear not only that a new age is upon us but that unity is to become ever wider, ever closer. Africa and the Africans have a golden opportunity to pool their undivided energies and put to use their vast resources as the United States has done; for plain common sense and a glance at a map of the world in the jet age proclaim the essential unity of the African continent, and to the impartial observer the unity of Africa is only a matter of time. As long ago as 1917, Dr. Kwegyir Aggrey of Ghana said, "It is not too far distant when in all things African, Africa will be truly represented by her sons and daughters." Yet forty years is not such a long time in colonial Africa— not when one considers how far Africa has come in the last forty years, or in the last ten years, for that matter, during which the African Personality has begun to assume its full stature in the international community of independent nations. And as recently as 1961, Julius Nyerere of Tanganyika spoke the following prophetic words before the General Assembly of the United Nations:

The unity of the whole of Africa is our ambition, and we know that it has to be a unity based on the free decision of independent African states. With a united Africa we believe that not only will the danger of conflict on our continent be avoided, but also that we shall be strengthened in the battle which each of the states is now waging—the fight against poverty, against ignorance, which we are inheriting from a colonial system. Cooperation across national boundaries would be easy if these were secondary to our membership in a united African community. . . . Every free African state has already spoken in favor of some form of unity or another. We are merely adding our voices to theirs, and our efforts to theirs, toward unity on our continent. We believe that organic unity will be achieved, but we also recognize that it will be the more easily achieved the more quickly we can move in that direction.

IV

Positive Neutralism and Nonalignment

As the African Personality asserts itself on the continent of Africa by searching for unity, so it asserts itself beyond its borders, among the nations of the world, by following a policy of positive neutrality and nonalignment. The two are, of course, related, as domestic and foreign policies so often are; but the latter policy is an unusual one in many ways, for it emerges from, and is consistent with, Africa's unique position as a continent not only struggling to free itself from European domination but unwilling to exchange a Western form of domination for an Eastern one. Positive neutralism, however, strikes many people as a contradiction in terms, especially since neutrality is usually associated with passivity. But the African policy is neither negative nor passive, as we shall see, although its development from earlier concepts may at first make it seem so. Dr. Kwame Nkrumah has said of positive neutralism, for example, that it does not "imply that the Government of Ghana will be a mere silent spectator of world events. On the contrary, the Government of Ghana will continue to take positive steps through the United Nations to promote and maintain peace and security among all nations. We shall always adopt whatever positive policies will do most to safeguard our independence and world peace." And President Modibo Keita of Mali has described the policy as "the refusal of a nation to lose its personality in a world where assimilation is the objective of every great power." These two statements may seem to stress the negative, yet they take into account the two great realities, so to speak, of our time— the United Nations and the Cold War—and so revise the traditional concept of neutrality from an instrument of passivity into one of activity.

Yet, since neutralism has always been a profoundly controversial subject, arousing the most inflamed passions in those already committed to participation in a conflict of one kind or another, actual or ideological, perhaps I should say a few words about it. From the fifth century B.C., when the Melians found themselves caught between Sparta and Athens, until the twentieth century A.D., when nations like India find themselves enmeshed in the struggle between East and West, the controversy has periodically flared up—and particularly since the outbreak of the Korean War in 1950. Before then, I think it is safe to say that the two main types of neutrality had been *ad hoc* neutrality and traditional neutrality. The former might be defined as the neutrality of a third power toward states involved in conflict—for example, Ireland and Portugal during World War II; the latter as the pursuit of a continuous basic policy—for example, Switzerland or, until 1917, the United States. Until World War II and the subsequent establishment of the United Nations, neutrality was usually regarded as a luxury that could be afforded only by those states which had the strength to resist attacks from one or more of the belligerents, were so strategically located that they could defend themselves either with ease or at cost to the aggressor, or had been guaranteed neutrality, as it were, by the belligerents themselves for reasons of mutual convenience. Those states which based their neutrality on anything else were clearly living in a world of illusion, which was all too often shattered. It is ironic, as a matter of fact, to recall that Belgium, which committed aggression against the young Congo Republic in July, 1960, had at least twice before tried to save herself from aggression by relying on protestations of neutrality. This attitude, in its manifestation, not only transformed Belgium into a fool's paradise, into which German tanks and planes burst one morning in May, 1940, but hastened the fall of Belgium's own allies. By failing to understand her own true interests, Belgium injured both herself and her allies.

With such illusory forms of neutrality, the policy of positive neutrality and nonalignment has nothing in common, for it has continually concerned itself with political realities. In fact, it may be said to have been born in response to political realities, one of which, curiously enough, was the powerful current of thought that has consistently held, ever since the outbreak of the Korean War in 1950, that neutralism is not only outmoded but impossible. For when the United States and the Soviet Union took opposite sides in the war between the North and South Koreans, countries like India, which followed an avowed policy of neutrality, had to be careful, whatever the merits of the situation, not to incur the wrath of either of the two great protagonists. And yet they were being placed in the most difficult of situations simply because the protagonists themselves seemed to make it impossible for neutral nations to remain neutral.

On the Communist side, for example, there were many declarations of policy in the Soviet Union that echoed the eras of Lenin and Stalin, revealing the view that he who is not for us is against us. Perhaps the most vivid expression was contained in a speech made by Mao Tse-tung of China on July 1, 1949, entitled "On the Peoples' Democratic Dictatorship." It was in commemoration of the twenty-eighth anniversary of the founding of the Chinese Communist Party, and he was speaking of the conflict between "reactionaries" and "revolutionaries": "In front of a wild beast you cannot show the slightest cowardice. We must learn from Wu Sung. . . . To Wu Sung, the tiger on the Chingyang would eat people all the same whether they were provocative or not. You either kill the tiger or are eaten by it; there is no third choice." (Wu Sung was one of 108 heroes in the Chinese book *All Men Are Brothers,* and he killed a tiger with his bare hands.) So, too, with the Soviet Union: It has found fault with the policy of neutrality, and, as its overt hostility toward President Tito of Yugoslavia has indicated, it maintains that there can be no neutrality on the issue of capitalism versus Communism.

However, it must be said that Communist China's attitude toward positive neutralism is much more rigid than the Soviet Union's. While the Soviet Government is prepared to countenance a policy of positive neutrality and also coexistence as such, China has always been suspicious of countries following such policies. The recent border conflict between China and India may well have stemmed from the basic Chinese suspicion of India as a nonaligned country, as well as China's view of India as a "bourgeois," semicapitalist nation ideologically inclined toward the West rather than the East. There is no doubt that the India-China conflict did put to the test the whole policy of nonalignment. While there is bound to be an agonizing reappraisal of this policy by the Indian Government, I doubt whether the foreign policy of India will undergo any drastic change. I suspect, however, that India will refuse to support any Chinese causes and will remain basically hostile to the Peking Government for some time to come.

In the West, there have been equally strong opinions that neutralism is no longer tenable in the present ideological conflict. As a matter of fact, the late Secretary Dulles at one time raised this view nearly to the level of official Western policy; in 1956, he stated that the United States's mutual-security treaties with forty-two nations should "abolish, as between parties, the principle of neutrality which pretends that a nation can best gain safety for itself by being indifferent to the fate of others. This has increasingly become an obsolete conception, and, except under very special circumstances, it is an immoral and shortsighted conception." Although the Kennedy Administration has since discarded this view, it seems, nonetheless, to linger on in the psyche of the Western nations. It appears so frequently, and in such a variety of contexts, that one could easily become convinced of an ulterior purpose—to "permit" the uncommitted nations to pursue a policy of neutrality in order to soothe the feelings of the Afro-Asians, who do not like to be reminded of the fact that they are, in the Western view, dependent upon the West. In this context, "neutralism" becomes an artificial but necessary screen that is erected by general consent to protect a pro-Western country from attack, either diplomatic or propagandistic, by the other side—a device as indefinable but as generally accepted as that which confers status on a Frenchman's mistress. It has even provided material for the American comedian Mort Sahl, who has asked his audiences, "A neutral country, did you say? Is it one of our neutrals or one of theirs?"

Such were the views of neutralism in the capitals of both the Eastern and Western power blocs at the time that Ghana achieved her independence on March 6, 1957, and the fact that these views have, publicly at least, been modified in the last five years is in itself a tribute to the growing force of positive neutralism. The new neutralism had, however, been foreshadowed in the final communiqué of the Bandung Conference, in April, 1955, just as that had, in turn, developed from the Indian predicament in the Korean War of 1950–53. According to the communiqué:

All nations should have the right freely to choose their own political and economic systems and their own way of life in conformity with the purposes and principles of the Charter of the United Nations. . . . Nations should practice tolerance and live together in peace with one another as good neighbors and develop friendly cooperation on the basis of the following principles: abstention from the use of arrangements of collective defense to serve the particular interests of any of the big powers.

But the role Africa would play did not become clear until after Ghana had achieved independence two years later.

Ghana's contribution to the concept of neutrality has, in essence, been to provide it with a new attribute. The announcement at the first Conference of Independent African States, in April, 1958, when delegates expressed their common desire to pursue a foreign policy "with a view to safeguarding the hard-won independence, sovereignty, and territorial integrity of the participating states," deplored "the division of the greater part of the world into two antagonistic blocs," and affirmed certain fundamental principles, among which were loyalty to the United Nations and adherence to the principles enumerated at the Bandung Conference. The Accra Conference also affirmed its conviction that all participating governments "shall avoid being committed to any action which might entangle them to the detriment of their interest and freedom." This policy of nonalignment has since been followed by all the countries that attended the conference—all, that is, except Liberia, which has a traditional commitment to the United States, and Tunisia, which since her quarrel with France over the French base at Bizerte in July, 1961, has been moving in the direction of nonalignment. Of those African countries which became independent after the Accra Conference, only Guinea, Mali, Tanganyika, and, to some extent, Nigeria and Sierra Leone have followed a policy of nonalignment.

Later in 1958, Prime Minister Nkrumah made three statements that threw further light upon the concept of positive neutrality. On July 25, during an official visit to the United States, he told the U.S. House of Representatives: "Our policy is that of positive neutralism and nonalignment. This does not mean negative neutralism and should not be confused with the sort of neutralism which implies the suspension of judgment, but rather the conscientious exercise of it." In October, he expanded his views in an article published in the magazine *Western World:*

It has been made quite clear that so far as Ghana is concerned our policy toward all other nations will be based on one of independence and noninvolvement in power blocs. Our desire to keep clear of such blocs is motivated by the fact that only in such a situation can we hope to exert our influence in the world. We are quite aware that in terms of military or economic strength no action of ours can make any difference strategically or otherwise in the world balance of power. On the other hand, our involvement in power blocs might draw us into areas of conflict which have so far not strayed below the Sahara. In other words, we do not wish to be involved in these conflicts because we know that we cannot affect their outcome. Primarily, we believe that the peace of the world is served, not harmed, by keeping at least one great continent free from the strife and rivalry of military blocs. But this attitude of noninvolvement does not mean a suspension of judgment, nor does it imply indifference to the great issues of our day. It does not imply isolationism, neither is it anti-Western or anti-Eastern.

Also, in the October, 1958, issue of *Foreign Affairs,* Dr. Nkrumah wrote as follows:

Nonalignment can be understood only in the context of the present atomic arms race and the atmosphere of the Cold War. When we in Africa surveyed the industrial and military power concentrated behind the two great powers in the Cold War, we knew that no military or strategic act of ours could make one jot of difference to this balance of power, while our involvement might draw us into areas of conflict which so far have not spread below the Sahara. Our attitude, I imagine, is very much that of America looking at the disputes of Europe in the nineteenth century. We do not wish to be involved. . . . But this attitude of nonalignment does not imply indifference to the great issues of our day. . . . The greatest issue . . . is surely to see that there is a tomorrow. For Africans especially there is a particular tragedy in the risk of thermonuclear destruction. Our continent has come but lately to the threshold of the modern world. The opportunities for health and education and wider vision which other nations take for granted are barely within the reach of our people. And now they see the risk that all this richness of opportunity may be snatched away by destructive war. . . . It is not indifference that leads us to a policy of nonalignment. It is our belief that international blocs and rivalries exacerbate and do not solve disputes and that we must be free to judge issues on their merits and to look for solutions that are just and peaceful, irrespective of the powers involved. We do not wish to be in a position of condoning imperialism or aggression from any quarter. Powers which pursue policies of good will, cooperation, and constructive international action will always find us at their side. In fact, perhaps "nonalignment" is a misstatement of our attitude. We are firmly aligned with all the forces in the world that genuinely make for peace.

In pointing out that the attitude of the Ghana Government would seem "very much that of America looking at the disputes of Europe in the nineteenth century," President Nkrumah might well have echoed the words of George Washington, who, in his Farewell Address, said that Europe

> . . . has a set of primary interests which to us have no, or have a very remote, relation. Hence she must be engaged in frequent controversies, the causes of which are essentially foreign to our concerns. Hence, therefore, it must be unwise in us to implicate ourselves by artificial ties in the ordinary vicissitudes of her policies, or the ordinary combinations and collisions of her friendships and enmities. Our detached and distant situation invites and enables us to pursue a different course.

There are, however, certain clearly discernible differences between the situation of the fledgling United States and that of the newly independent states of Africa today. The advance of science has, at the very least, outmoded the type of isolationism that the United States pursued in its earlier years and formalized in the Monroe Doctrine. For when the Monroe Doctrine was proclaimed, on December 2, 1823, there were, of course, no tele-communications, rockets, or jet planes, and, most important of all, there was no United Nations. The Charter of the United Nations may, in fact, be said to be symbolic of the difference, for since it was signed, international relations have, to a large extent, been based on the concept of peaceful coexistence—a term that I think it might be useful to define, since it means so many things to so many people.

To establish a peaceful world, the architects of the United Nations envisaged a world organization open to all states regardless of political or ideological complexion. Therefore, Article 4 of the Charter declares that "membership in the United Nations is open to all other peace-loving states which accept the obligations contained in the Charter and, in the judgment of the organization, are able and willing to carry out these obligations." Thus the principle of the sovereign equality of all nations was upheld: It does not matter whether a state is ruled by elected representatives of the people, by a dictator, or by a military junta; it does not matter whether a state is large, medium, or small, whether it is capitalist or Communist. It should be possible for any kind of state to carry on normal diplomatic relations with other states in the world organization.

Every state has, to be sure, an inherent right, based on the exercise of its sovereignty, to refuse to recognize another state, and this right does open the concept of peaceful coexistence to challenge. So, too, though less strongly, does the possibility of regional arrangements, which were anticipated under Article 52 of the United Nations Charter. Although this article permits the formation of regional organizations, such as the Organization of American States, it states that any such arrangements must be made consistent with the purposes and principles of the Charter. Therefore, when the Organization of American States decided to expel Cuba from its membership—after the meeting of the foreign ministers of the American states at Punta del Este, Uruguay, in 1962—the question was immediately raised as to whether or not the decision was in accordance with the provisions of the Charter. In other words, should the principles of coexistence be upheld in a regional organization that already has its own rules made by, and acceptable to, its own members? In my opinion, mutual respect should form the basis for relations among nations; otherwise, hostility toward another regime because of its political, economic, or social system may eventually lead to armed conflict, to the attempt to destroy what one nation neither likes nor understands, probably out of fear, about another nation. Cuba's expulsion from the Organization of American States, therefore, might be viewed in that light. As one of my distinguished colleagues at the United Nations, Mr. Ahmad Shukairy of Saudi Arabia, once said at a meeting of the Political Committee of the General Assembly: "What is peaceful coexistence if we cannot accept the doctrines of others, the ideologies of others, the social orders of others, and the economic systems of others?"

It is, I think, reasonable to suggest that just as the Monroe Doctrine has been subtly modified by the realities of the United Nations Charter, so any African equivalent of the Monroe Doctrine today—that is, any policy that seeks to encourage the development of Africa free from the interference of foreign powers whose interests cannot be identical with those of the African states—must also take into account this one great fact of international life, the U.N. Charter. We tend to forget that the adoption of the Charter was an event of the utmost significance and that it has, in the years following its adoption, profoundly affected all phases of international relations, including the concept of neutrality and the nature of regional pacts. For if the Charter means anything, it means that mankind as a whole is at the dawn of a new era in international relations, an era in which a major war as a method of solving disputes has become outmoded. If this seems too optimistic a point of view, consider the fact that—despite the extraordinary scientific advances since

World War II in nuclear weapons, rockets, and manned satellites
—the so-called Cold War has not yet erupted into a full-scale
"hot war."

I have discussed these matters at some length in order to provide, from an African point of view, the context within which
positive neutralism has evolved: the signing of the U.N. Charter,
the division of the world into two great power blocs centered
about the United States and the Soviet Union, and the gradual
emergence of independent African states—the last of which,
occurring almost simultaneously with, and in response to, the
first two, has enabled Africa's statesmen to assess the past from
a fresh and unencumbered viewpoint. Positive neutralism, therefore, draws upon the experiences of the past, takes into account
the realities of the present, and is designed to help the international community to advance peacefully into the future. As a
doctrine, it is possible only within the framework of an international community in which the majority of nations, as they do
today, subscribe to the principles and purposes of the United Nations; as an expression of the African Personality, it seeks to avoid
entangling alliances with either East or West, for, as the past has
taught and the present is teaching, Africa can emerge—as it is
now surely but slowly emerging—only *between* rather than on
one side or the other of East and West. And as a force for peace,
both dynamic and strategic, it functions actively for peace—
that is, for peaceful progress and prosperity. There is, in short,
nothing passive about this form of neutrality, for it is directed toward the attainment of a state in which constant effort and re-
newal of effort are demanded of all nations, not simply a state in
which tension, conflict, or war is merely absent. As Africans
know only too well, freedom, independence, and prosperity must
not only be won by long and hard struggle and sacrifice but continue to be maintained and preserved by diligence and perse-
verance. Their form of neutrality, therefore, must be the object

of continual striving, since it is exercised in favor of peace; and peace, in turn, is in itself a condition of neutrality.

Since positive neutralism is a cornerstone of Ghana's foreign policy, it might be instructive, as a means of illustration and further definition, to examine past applications of the policy at the United Nations. Let us select three issues—Hungary, the reorganization of the United Nations Secretariat, and Cuba—to show how one African nation, Ghana, applied itself to resolving these problems. Two of them involved violence, bloodshed, and intervention, open or covert, by a foreign power; the third involved a drastic change in the post of the Secretary-General because of the Soviet proposal for a "troika."

The Hungarian situation first came before the General Assembly in November, 1956. Shortly before, the Hungarian people were reported to have revolted against their government; since the government appeared powerless to suppress the revolt, the Soviet Union, according to the reports, moved in troops and tanks to help the unpopular government put down the rebellion. It was this alleged Soviet intervention that led the United States and other Western countries to call for an emergency session of the General Assembly. After a heated debate, the Assembly decided to set up a special committee, which presented its report to the Eleventh Session of the General Assembly in September, 1957—six months after Ghana had been admitted to the United Nations. On the basis of the report, the General Assembly adopted a resolution which stated that since the Soviet Union had deprived the people of Hungary of their liberty and political independence and was responsible for other acts of repression, the United Nations condemned these acts.

The presentation of the committee's report confronted Ghana with the first major international question on which it was obliged to make a decision. On September 13, 1957, during the debate on the Hungarian situation, the representative of Ghana stated: "As a nation which has only recently achieved its independence, we have a vested interest in orderly international intercourse and the rule of law, and we would always vehemently protest in any instance in which it was clearly demonstrated that one country had used its superior military power to crush a movement for freedom in another country." The representative then went on to say that the delegation of Ghana would support the resolution on Hungary, but pointed out that "we would be sorely disappointed if the adoption of the resolution were to be interpreted by any side as a political victory or defeat. We are here concerned only with principles and the suffering of humanity, wherever that may be."

The task of the reorganization of the Secretariat of the United Nations had been assigned to a Committee of Experts, which, according to Resolution 1446 of the Fourteenth Session of the General Assembly in 1959, was "to work with the Secretary-General in reviewing the activities and the reorganization of the Secretariat with a view to effecting or proposing further measures designed to ensure maximum economy and efficiency in the Secretariat." I served on this Committee together with Mr. Omar Loutfi, then the Permanent Representative of the United Arab Republic (now Under-Secretary under U Thant), Mr. Guillaume Georges-Picot of France, Mr. Francisco Urrutia of Colombia, Mr. A. A. Fomin of the Soviet Union, Sir Harold Parker of the United Kingdom, Mr. C. S. Venkatachar of India, and Dr. Herman B. Wells (later replaced by Professor Leland M. Goodrich) of the United States.

The Committee of Experts was thus engaged in its work when Premier Nikita Khrushchev, Chairman of the Council of Ministers of the Soviet Union, raised the issue of the reorganization of the Secretariat in his statement before the General Assembly on September 23, 1960. The Russians had not been very happy with the handling of the Congo operations by Dag Hammarskjöld, and had come to the conclusion that the post of the

Secretary-General should be substituted by a triumvirate representing the three basic groups of states existing in the world—the socialist states, the nonaligned states, and the Allied Western states. According to Chairman Khrushchev, "there are no neutral men," and, therefore, the Secretary-General could not possibly be objective in his handling of issues that affect all member states. The Soviet Union also accused Hammarskjöld of being "a servant of the colonialists" and argued that the events of the world, especially those in the Congo at the time, had demonstrated the necessity of reorganizing the structure of the Secretariat and its management at the top level. In Khrushchev's view, the Secretariat did not reflect the change in the international balance of forces or take into account the emergence of a strong socialist world, the collapse of colonialism, and the emergence of a large number of nonaligned countries. The Soviet Union argued that by the adoption of the troika system, therefore, it would not be possible to favor this or that bloc of powers, and the decisions of the Security Council and the General Assembly would then be faithfully carried out by the Secretariat.

As was to be expected, the other great power, the United States, opposed this move with the valid argument that a change in the post of the Secretary-General would involve an amendment to the Charter, and that what was required in any case was one chief administrative officer at the helm of the Secretariat. The United States expressed its solid opposition to the troika proposal.

Ghana and other nonaligned countries did not take kindly to the open accusations leveled against the person of Secretary-General Hammarskjöld and other officials, although, on many occasions, we had had cause to complain about the way United Nations operations were being conducted in the Congo. The Soviet troika proposal took us all by surprise.

Therefore, when Chairman Khrushchev made his far-reaching proposal, the President of Ghana, who was then in New York, immediately decided that the nonaligned states should take a position of their own. At a luncheon given in his honor by the United Nations Correspondents Association in September, 1960, Osagyefo Dr. Kwame Nkrumah proposed that there should be no change in the post of Secretary-General, but that there should be three Deputy Secretaries-General who would form a kind of cabinet presided over by the Secretary-General. Ghana's position was definitely in defense of the Charter of the United Nations, but our view was that account had to be taken of the prevailing circumstances in international life. If the Secretary-General was to carry out his functions properly, then he would have to consult regularly, and work in cooperation with, his top advisers, who may be designated as deputies but in fact are under-secretaries.

The idea of a cabinet system at the top echelons of the Secretariat was strongly supported by Premier Nehru of India, who, in his address before the Fifteenth Session of the General Assembly, made it clear that the troika proposal of the Soviet Union would not work. Thus, the nonaligned states became united in their search for a compromise that would not involve an amendment of the Charter and would avoid weakening the executive functions of the Secretary-General, who, after all, has overriding responsibility for the running of the Secretariat under Articles 97–101 of the Charter.

Article 97 stipulates that the Secretary-General "shall be the chief administrative officer of the Organization." Article 98 states that "the Secretary-General shall act in that capacity in all meetings of the General Assembly, of the Security Council, of the Economic and Social Council, and of the Trusteeship Council, and shall perform such other functions as are entrusted to him by these organs. The Secretary-General shall make an annual report to the General Assembly on the work of the Organization."

These two articles, together with Article 101, deal with the purely administrative functions of the Secretary-General. But Article 99 confers on him the right "to bring to the attention of the Security Council any matter which in his opinion may threaten the maintenance of international peace and security," and Article 100 emphasizes the international character of his post and the fact that no member state shall exert influence on him or any of his staff in the discharge of their duties.

Therefore, the nonaligned states put their weight solidly behind the Charter and appealed to the Soviet Union not to press its troika system. We have argued that the responsibilities of the Secretary-General go beyond the concept of a nonpolitical civil servant and that, because he may take stands of a political and controversial nature, there was need for adequate and regular consultations between the Secretary-General and his top advisers, whose views must reflect the realities of international life.

Consequently, in the Committee of Experts dealing with the reorganization of the Secretariat, I pressed the proposal for Deputy Secretaries-General, and in this I was ably supported by Omar Loutfi and C. S. Venkatachar. Hammarskjöld agreed to the idea of a cabinet system, and a month before his untimely death he conferred with the three of us and proposed that there should be five or six under-secretaries—drawn from Africa, Asia, Europe, Latin America, the Soviet Union, and the United States —instead of three to form the Secretary-General's cabinet.

Of course, the issue of a troika persisted after Hammarskjöld's death, and for some time it seemed as if the United Nations was going to do without a Secretary-General. But the nonaligned states were determined to press the idea of one Secretary-General as defined by the Charter, assisted by a cabinet.

In retrospect, it is satisfying to realize that U Thant, who became the new Secretary-General of the world organization, had taken part in our deliberations as Ambassador of Burma.

Here, then, is an instance where positive neutralism as an active policy has contributed tremendously to the maintenance of peace and the settling of a Cold War issue.

The Cuban complaint of October, 1960, "regarding the various plans of aggression and acts of intervention being executed by the government of the United States of America against the Republic of Cuba, constituting a manifest violation of territorial integrity, sovereignty, and independence and a clear threat to international peace and security"—this was a third issue on which Ghana and other nonaligned nations had to act circumspectly. Here was a small country, Cuba, which felt that a large one, the United States, was determined to destroy it, and under normal circumstances it should have had the full support of all other small countries. But Cuba's accusation against the United States was a grave one, and it was utterly repudiated by the United States, which argued not only that Cuba had become a Communist stronghold but that it was Cuban exiles who were acting to overthrow the government of Fidel Castro. The Cuban issue could not be considered simply as a Cold War issue of itself, but the fact that the Soviet Union stood forth as the champion of the Cuban case against the United States made tension run high indeed. Therefore, nonaligned countries like Ethiopia, Ghana, India, Indonesia, Sudan, United Arab Republic, and Yugoslavia were looked upon as possible mediators, and we all made every effort to be as objective as possible by counseling nonintervention.

Most of the representatives of the nonaligned countries who took the floor spoke, as I remember, in favor of an earlier resolution passed during the Fourth Session of the General Assembly, in 1949. This had called upon all states "to refrain from threats or acts, direct or indirect, aimed at impairing the freedom, independence, or integrity of any state, or at fomenting civil strife and subverting the will of the people in any state." Speaking on behalf of Ghana, I said:

> Ghana has cordial relations with both the United States and Cuba. Apart from the mutual esteem and the friendly relations existing between Ghana and Cuba, on the one hand, and Ghana and the United States, on the other, there is a feeling of kinship all around due to the fact that in both Cuba and the United States

there are large numbers of people of African descent whose welfare and progress cannot but engage our attention.

In April, 1961, as reports reached the United Nations that Cuba had been attacked by an invading force from outside Cuba, I spoke before the Political Committee of the General Assembly:

> The delegation of Ghana is not in a position to be a judge in this matter, but we are painfully aware of the fact that there has indeed been an attack on Cuba from outside by planes which have taken off from places outside Cuba; and, in fact, Guatemala and the United States have been cited by the Foreign Minister of Cuba in his statement before this committee. We are painfully aware that Cubans have been killed in this escapade. My delegation expresses the sympathy of the people of Ghana to the families of those who have lost their lives in Cuba. . . . We therefore ask the Assembly to urge that all direct or indirect assistance for the armed intervention be discontinued and that, in accordance with the Charter of the United Nations, the parties concerned settle this dispute by peaceful means, a settlement which will lead to pacification and enable the Cuban peoples to work out their own destiny in complete freedom.

Although the Assembly did not adopt any resolution on the Cuban question, the debate was sufficient to emphasize the necessity for nonintervention in Cuba by any outside power.

The later, and far more serious, Cuban crisis of October, 1962 —brought about by the United States "blockade" of Cuba in response to the installation of Soviet missile bases there—deserves some mention. This crisis nearly engulfed the world in a nuclear holocaust. Quick action was needed to save humanity from destruction. The nonaligned states at the United Nations played a decisive role. Mahmoud Riad (of the U.A.R.) and I became their unofficial spokesmen at the Security Council—in getting U Thant, Acting Secretary-General, to intervene between the two great powers. In the end, common sense prevailed. Khrushchev and Kennedy reached an agreement that quickly averted the danger of war over Cuba. The bases were dismantled and the missiles taken back to the Soviet Union. The United States then lifted the "quarantine" or "blockade" of Cuba. And what remained was the still-unresolved bad relations between Cuba and the United States and the Latin American countries.

In all three of the cases cited, I have endeavored to show that positive neutralism is much more active a policy than that usually connoted by the word "neutrality." Any country that pursues such a policy of positive neutralism and nonalignment must be prepared to work hard, for it must undertake the most assiduous and objective analyses in order to decide how that country may, by word and deed, best aid the cause of peace. And as long as the Soviet Union and the United States assume antipodal positions on world problems and attempt to entice into their orbits any number of other countries, so long will there be a need for a group of countries to remain outside the two camps—a group of countries that will approach international issues as objectively as possible and speak out for justice, morality, and human rights. Here, then, is Africa's opportunity to serve, and that is the reason I hope that all African nations will adopt the policy of positive neutralism and nonalignment.

There are, of course, a number of ways in which neutral or nonaligned nations may bring their collective weight and pressure upon the great powers in their active campaign for peace. One of the courses that lie open has been outlined by President Nkrumah of Ghana in a speech to the U.N. General Assembly on September 23, 1960:

> It is essential that we on the African continent take positive steps to isolate ourselves so far as is possible from the effects of nuclear warfare. One of the first and most practical steps which could be taken in this regard is to prevent any state having nuclear weapons from possessing military bases on the African continent. This is

one of the main reasons why the Government of Ghana believes that no African state should enter into an alliance of a military nature with any outside power. Any such alliance not only involves the state concerned in the risk of being drawn into nuclear warfare, it also endangers the security of the neighboring African states. Fallout is no respecter of frontiers, and a declaration of neutrality cannot save the people of any African state from nuclear poisoning once atomic war is introduced into the African continent. A military alliance with any atomic power is, therefore, in the view of the Government of Ghana, a threat to the security of Africa and world peace. The Government of Ghana therefore feels that it is its duty to support all measures taken within the framework of the United Nations Charter and in collaboration with like-minded African states to prevent the establishment or maintenance of military bases on the African continent. . . . I hope the great powers who possess atomic weapons will appreciate our feelings in this regard and will voluntarily relinquish any bases that they may at present possess in Africa. I believe that it is the duty of the United Nations to encourage the growth of zones free from nuclear warfare. A start in this policy must be made somewhere, and I therefore make the positive proposal that whatever other steps may be taken to effect nuclear disarmament, a start should be made by all nuclear powers agreeing to keep Africa out of their nuclear-warfare plans.

Dr. Nkrumah's proposal has certain similarities, as a matter of fact, to the Rapacki Plan, first proposed to the General Assembly on October 3, 1957, by Adam Rapacki, the Foreign Minister of Poland and, in my opinion, one of the outstanding statesmen of our times. He suggested that an atom-free zone be established in Central Europe—a zone that would cover East Germany, West Germany, Poland, and Czechoslovakia. The Nkrumah proposal, however, was confined to the continent of Africa, was not linked in any way with the internal problems of Europe and Africa, and sought, in effect, a solution to large world problems by indirect methods—by making a start "somewhere," as President Nkrumah put it. The establishment of a nuclear-free zone in Africa would, if honored by the nuclear powers, clearly lessen potential areas of conflict; it would, in fact, run the risk of "contaminating" an unhealthy situation with healthy elements. But there is a tried and trusty procedure for ameliorating even the most apparently hopeless situations in international affairs: Identify the main elements, separate out the positive elements, no matter how small, and then encourage the latter to grow and expand until they begin to flower. The proponents of positive neutralism, noting that Africa is at the moment largely a nuclear-free zone (despite the series of French tests in the Sahara), proposed to preserve that continent in an international agreement; they thereby indicated a course of action that could result in a reduction of international tensions and does, indeed, offer a solid foundation for further progress toward world peace. It is significant, I think, that no great power opposed the resolution offered by Ghana and fourteen other African countries and passed by the General Assembly that Africa should be declared a denuclearized zone. The General Assembly passed the resolution to this effect with an overwhelming majority, without a single dissenting vote.

Although positive neutralism is, as I have described it, a constructive challenge to the great powers, proposed by the states of Africa in the interests of peaceful coexistence, the great powers, for their part, are not at all enthusiastic about it. In fact, they are doing all they can to persuade, woo, entice, even threaten the nations that espouse positive neutralism, and such tactics make it very difficult for a number of nations which, because of economic disabilities, cannot maintain a vigorously independent foreign policy.

A case in point is the attitude displayed by the major powers toward the heads of state of the nonaligned countries who met in Belgrade, Yugoslavia, September 1–6, 1961. (The following states were represented: Afghanistan, Algeria, Burma, Cambodia,

Ceylon, Congo (Léopoldville), Cuba, Cyprus, Ethiopia, Ghana, Guinea, India, Indonesia, Iraq, Lebanon, Mali, Morocco, Nepal, Saudi Arabia, Somalia, Sudan, Tunisia, U.A.R., Yemen, and Yugoslavia.) For it soon became clear that neither of the two Cold War antagonists looked with favor upon a world grouping that might easily become a powerful third force; each, quite obviously, preferred to have the nonaligned powers commit themselves to its respective ideologies. The Soviet Union, however, seems more inclined than the United States to accept the idea of a neutral grouping, since it at least makes it easier for her to know which countries are not on her side. The United States, on the other hand, accepts the idea of such a grouping with reluctance, for she seems to maintain a deep-rooted suspicion that since most of the countries concerned were once colonial territories under European domination, it must logically follow that they tend to be more sympathetic to the Soviet Union. In fact, the leaders of the United States expressed great disappointment that the Belgrade Conference did not condemn the Soviet Union for breaking the 1958 moratorium on nuclear tests, yet overlooked one important detail: Every head of state who spoke at the conference after the first Soviet explosion expressed both shock and regret that there had been a resumption of nuclear testing.

It is my belief that the attitude of the United States toward the Belgrade Conference was, in general, unjustified. The conference was called simply because of the prevailing international tensions, which had, in turn, been caused by, and then reinforced, the rigid positions taken by the Soviet Union and the United States in regard to Berlin, Cuba, and the Congo; the heads of state of the nonaligned countries were making an attempt to bring together the two great powers without even a limited war. Anyone who was at Belgrade, as I was, could not mistake the genuine desires of the twenty-five heads of state to effect a breakthrough. Under the difficult circumstances, the

first and most necessary step was to appeal to the leaders of the
Soviet Union and the United States—not to issue a condemnation of either one of them for an act recently committed. In
any case, I do not see how a king, president, emperor, or woman
prime minister (Madame Bandanarike of Ceylon) could stoop
to using condemnatory words at such a high-level conference.
Actually, the conference decided to send two missions—one to
Moscow and one to Washington. President Nkrumah and Premier Nehru delivered a letter to Chairman Khrushchev; and
President Sukarno of Indonesia and President Keita of Mali delivered a similar message to President Kennedy. Both urged the
great powers to resume negotiations to remove the danger of war.
That the heads of state were really firm in their views on world
problems was quite clear from the communiqué issued at Belgrade, and they particularly emphasized that nonalignment is a
positive rather than a passive policy:

> The participants in the conference consider that, under present
> conditions, the existence and the activities of nonaligned countries
> in the interest of peace are one of the more important factors for
> safeguarding world peace. . . . [They] consider it essential that
> the nonaligned countries should participate in solving outstanding
> international issues concerning peace and security in the world as
> none of them can remain unaffected by or indifferent to these
> issues. . . . [They] consider that the further extension of the non-
> committed area of the world constitutes the only possible and in-
> dispensable alternative to the policy of total division of the world
> into blocs and the intensification of Cold War policies.

For Africa, the spirit of Belgrade provided a good omen. The
desire of African states to pursue an independent foreign policy
was thereby fortified by the calling into existence, as it were, of
a group of nonaligned countries even beyond the borders of
Africa itself—countries such as Yugoslavia, India, Cambodia, and

Indonesia. The African struggle to become completely free from domination—physical, economic, ideological, and cultural—will be won, I believe, by means of our policy of positive neutrality. It is only by an honest implementation of this policy that the African Personality can continue to realize itself and so make African contributions to the United Nations meaningful.

V

Africa and the United Nations

In 1941, at the height of World War II, Winston Churchill and Franklin D. Roosevelt agreed upon the need for an international organization—provisional, if necessary, until a permanent system of general security could be established—to bring about the disarmament and effective control of aggressive nations. This need was emphasized at a conference of foreign ministers of the United Kingdom, the United States, the Union of Soviet Socialist Republics, and the Republic of China, held in October, 1943, when the delegates "recognized the necessity of establishing at the earliest practicable date a general international organization, based on the principle of sovereign equality of all peaceloving states, and open to membership by all states, large and small, for the maintenance of international peace and security." Soon thereafter, in confirmation, the three Allied leaders—Churchill, Roosevelt, and Stalin—agreed, at Teheran, "to seek the cooperation and active participation of all nations, large and small, whose peoples in heart and mind are dedicated, as are our peoples, to the elimination of tyranny and slavery, oppression and intolerance." Between August 20 and October 7, 1944, at Dumbarton Oaks, the proposed world organization took definite shape, and between April and June, 1945, the time of Germany's surrender, the Charter of the United Nations was established.

The Preamble of the Charter sums up the thoughts and aspirations of its founders, to establish a world without war:

We the peoples of the United Nations determined to save succeeding generations from the scourge of war, which twice in our lifetime has brought untold sorrow to mankind, and to reaffirm faith in fundamental human rights, in the dignity and worth of the human person, in the equal rights of men and women and of nations large and small, and to establish conditions under which justice and respect for the obligations arising from treaties and other sources of international law can be maintained, and to promote social progress and better standards of life in larger freedom, AND FOR THESE ENDS to practice tolerance and live together in peace with one another as good neighbors, and to unite our strength to maintain international peace and security, and to ensure, by the acceptance of principles and the institution of methods that armed force shall not be used, save in the common interest, and to employ international machinery for the promotion of the economic and social advancement of all peoples, HAVE RESOLVED TO COMBINE OUR EFFORTS TO ACCOMPLISH THESE AIMS. Accordingly, our respective governments, through representatives assembled in the city of San Francisco, who have exhibited their full powers found to be in good and due form, have agreed to the present Charter of the United Nations and do hereby establish an international organization to be known as the United Nations.

From the Preamble, as well as from the Charter itself, it becomes evident that all nations, and indeed humanity itself, had become sick of wars, that there was a deep and universal longing for peace, and that the new organization provided the best hope of engaging in international cooperation, practicing a philosophy of international morality, and thereby ensuring the complete elimination of war from the world. The quest for international peace was, in a word, to be attained by international cooperation in the economic, social, and cultural fields—by the respect, that is, for human rights and fundamental freedoms.

The universality of membership of the United Nations was not really in doubt, although those who met at San Francisco were largely unaware of the tremendous forces of liberation soon to be sweeping through Africa. Now, however, it has become so fashionable to speak of Africa and the African point of view in the United Nations that it is often forgotten that as recently as June, 1945, when the Charter of the United Nations was signed, Africa was still the forgotten continent. True, provisions were made in the Charter for the colonial territories of Africa; but the provisions were the result of the mandate system inherited by the United Nations from the old League of Nations, not of any widespread realization that the political awakening of the peoples of Africa was close at hand. In fact, the prospect of internationalizing the colonial problem in Africa seemed repugnant to Winston Churchill, for it is reported that during a discussion about the future of dependent territories while the three Allied leaders were meeting at Yalta, Churchill asked Stalin how he would feel about a proposal to internationalize the Crimea as a holiday resort. Evidently, then, the future of the colonies was regarded by the British, even at that time, as a subject outside the scope of international concern—let alone international supervision. But in those days, any discussions about colonial problems centered on Asia; it was generally accepted, by even the best-informed delegations at San Francisco, that the political independence of the African continent was at least fifty years away, if attainable at all, and the delegates seem to have consigned the problem to their future grandchildren. It has transpired, however, that the same men who seem to have dismissed the problem for posterity to consider were themselves finally obliged to wrestle with it. Little did they realize that Africa was in no waiting mood, that in the very same year, 1945, Kwame Nkrumah was at Manchester, England, as joint secretary of the Fifth Pan-African Conference (the most crucial one of all and the last to be held outside the continent of Africa).

What the fathers of the United Nations Charter did, then, was simply to confine the fate of non-self-governing territories—since the word "colonies" was, even then, unpopular, "non-self-governing" was proposed by the Chinese delegation as a compromise—to a single article of the Charter, Article 73 in Chapter XI. The pertinent paragraphs read as follows:

Members of the United Nations which have or assume responsibilities for the administration of territories whose peoples have not yet attained a full measure of self-government recognize the principle that the interests of the inhabitants of these territories are paramount, and accept as a sacred trust the obligation to promote to the utmost, within the system of international peace and security established by the present Charter, the well-being of the inhabitants of these territories, and, to this end:

a. to ensure, with due respect for the culture of the peoples concerned, their political, economic, social, and educational advancement, their just treatment, and their protection against abuses;

b. to develop self-government, to take due account of the political aspirations of the peoples, and to assist them in the progressive development of their free political institutions, according to the particular circumstances of each territory and its peoples and their varying stages of advancement;

c. to further international peace and security;

d. to promote constructive measures of development, to encourage research, and to cooperate with one another and, when and where appropriate, with specialized international bodies with a view to the practical achievement of the social, economic, and scientific purposes set forth in this Article; and

e. to transmit regularly to the Secretary-General for information purposes, subject to such limitation as security and constitutional consideration may require, statistical and other information of a technical nature relating to economic, social, and educational conditions in the territories for which they are respectively responsible other than those territories to which Chapters XII and XIII apply.

The remainder of the dependent territories—those which had not been colonies of the Allied powers—became known as trust territories. They were, in fact, the former colonies of the defeated Axis powers, which, between World Wars I and II, had had the status of mandates of the League of Nations. In accordance with Chapter XII of the Charter, these were placed under the international trusteeship system of the United Nations, and trusteeship agreements were then signed between the designated administering authority, on the one hand, and the United Nations, on the other. In this way, various African territories, as well as former Japanese territories in the Pacific, were placed under United Nations Trusteeship, and as trust territories they were not only inspected every three years by visiting missions from the United Nations, but also given the right to present petitions directly to the United Nations. So Britain became the administering authority for British Togoland, the Northern and Southern British Cameroons, and Tanganyika; France for French Togoland and the French Cameroons; and Belgium for Ruanda-Urundi. One exception, the territory of South-West Africa, I shall deal with later, since it poses special and complex problems.

Such, in brief, were the two methods by which the architects of the United Nations disposed, as it were, of the colonial question in 1945. If, however, it can be said that the United Nations Charter, like every man-made legal instrument, is an arbitrarily conceived device imposed in the name of civilization upon the organic but essentially anarchic flow of life, then it is susceptible to errors and faults. The main fault is simply this: that those who were attempting to draft a document that would lay claim to universal representation left out a whole continent, an entire dimension of the world—Africa and the African peoples. Consequently, when the time came for the document to withstand the test of practice and experience, it turned out that the claim to universality could not be entirely substantiated. But although the tensions between East and West precluded the possibility of the

Charter's being revised, and indeed still do, the flow of life could hardly be denied. As a result, Africa's growing momentum toward independence, her life-force, so to speak, has reached the proportions of a flood; but, first, it had to discover minor apertures in the wall of the Charter, seep through the foundations, and gradually widen the breach until the torrent came pouring through. That point may be said to have been reached about 1958, only thirteen years after the signing of the Charter in San Francisco.

One of the small chinks in the wall turned out, soon after the United Nations was formed, to be Article 87(b) of the Charter, which states that the General Assembly and the Trusteeship Council may accept petitions from the trust territories and, in consultation with the administering authority, examine them. This provision, which did not pertain to the non-self-governing territories, undoubtedly stemmed from the fact that these were "trust" territories—that is, territories that must eventually graduate to independence, according to Chapter XII of the Charter. Hence, it was not long before that right to petition began to be used by many individuals who wished to convince United Nations delegates that they had something important to say about this or that trust territory, but it was, naturally enough, the African petitioners who produced the greatest effect upon the delegates. The first African petitioner to be heard by the United Nations was Sylvanus Olympio, the late President of Togo, who came before the Trusteeship Council in 1947 to plead—unsuccessfully, as it turned out—for the unification of the former British Togoland (now part of Ghana) and the former French Togoland (now Togo). The attitude of the delegates at that time has been recalled, twelve years later, by an observer of the United Nations:

> We heard that there was a petitioner coming from Africa and didn't know quite what to expect. None of the delegates knew much about Africa, and I sincerely believe that many of them ex-

pected someone to come rushing into the Council in a leopard skin and accompanied by a rumble of drums. Instead of which in strolled Sylvanus Olympio in his natty business suit. The delegates may not have known it, but they were seeing, for the first time, the shape of things to come.

Although they found their task difficult at first, the petitioners learned more about the international community as the years went by, and they were not slow in acquiring the tactics of influencing delegates and thereby affecting decisions and resolutions. The delegates, in turn, began to learn more about Africa and her problems, to establish friendships with African representatives, and to revise some of their earlier prejudices and ideas. Therefore, it is not surprising that resolutions on the future status of Cameroon, Tanganyika, and the former Ruanda-Urundi embodied ideas proposed by the petitioners who came before the United Nations. And the destinies of many of these individual petitioners have indeed proved as dramatic as any imagined by a novelist: President Olympio was assassinated in January, 1963; Um Nyobe of the Cameroons was shot dead by French security forces and lies under concrete at a mission station; Julius Nyerere of Tanganyika became the first Prime Minister (and later the President) of his country; John Kale of Uganda died in a plane crash; Jariretundu Kozonguizi of South-West Africa traveled to Peking and then to London, where he continues to fight for the independence of his country; and Felix Moumié, leader of the Union des Populations du Cameroun, was poisoned with thallium in Geneva, Switzerland, after he failed to persuade the United Nations to hold elections in his country prior to independence. There have been many others, but it was such men as these who, whether they rose with their people or fell in the struggle for freedom, helped to make Africa's cause known before the United Nations.

The case of the other dependent territories—that is, those which were not trust territories—has been different, and the reason, curiously enough, is simply that they were the colonies of the victorious powers of World War II. These powers were, of course, the ones who framed the Charter of the United Nations; in so doing, they retained control of their own colonies, yet placed the colonies of the defeated powers, as I have said, under international trusteeship. As a result, the so-called trust territories, at least in the eyes of African nationalists from non-self-governing territories, appeared to be the privileged ones, for they had, in their right of petition, an international platform from which to air their grievances and propose their ideas and, in the visiting missions, reasonably impartial and objective supervisors. All the non-self-governing territories seemed to have as a basis for appeal —despite Article 1 of the Charter, which specifically mentions "the principle of equal rights and self-determination of peoples" —was the famous Article 73(e), quoted earlier, and that made no provision for transmitting information on *political* conditions to the United Nations. However, had the original conception of the relationship between the United Nations and the non-self-governing territories been realized—that is, that all non-self-governing territories should be placed under international trusteeship—there would, of course, have existed a clearly marked procedure by which such territories could have advanced, stage by stage, toward self-government and independence. It did not occur so smoothly, for the road was virtually blocked; and if a non-self-governing territory were to achieve its independence, it had to be through struggle and suffering, as Kwame Nkrumah of Ghana, Jomo Kenyatta of Kenya, Habib Bourguiba of Tunisia, Joshua Nkomo of Southern Rhodesia, Nnamdi Azikiwe of Nigeria, and Hastings Banda of Nyasaland can testify.

It is difficult for those Africans fighting for freedom to understand the motivations of the men who drafted and endorsed Chapter XI of the Charter. Yet the reasons were complex, if not completely ingenuous, and some of them Wilfred Benson, until recently United Nations resident representative in Ghana, has provided:

> The United States had to move with caution [at San Francisco in 1945] in view of the position of the defense interests to measures that might weaken the United States's hold over the Japanese islands of the Pacific. The United Kingdom established a claim to the paternity of Chapter XI by presenting principles of general policy. The Soviet Union was conservative, proposing measures limiting the role of the United Nations in ways which might have been agreeable to American admirals. More came from Australia, which had been active in promoting the idea of a common responsibility for the advancement of the peoples of the Pacific.*

(Lest the reader is surprised by the recollection that Britain and Australia took such progressive positions on colonial questions, we should recall that both countries then had Labour administrations, which were far less reactionary on such matters than the Conservative administrations which followed.)

Still, the Charter had been signed, and the non-self-governing territories had to make the best of it. But just as Article 87(b) had proved a weak point for the trust territories to concentrate upon, so Article 73(e) eventually provided the non-self-governing territories with their opening; for it required of the administering authorities the regular transmission to the United Nations Secretary-General of "statistical and other information of a technical nature relating to economic, social, and educational conditions" in the territories whose peoples "had not yet attained a full measure of self-government." Therefore, the first step was to make sure that such regulations were faithfully obeyed and carried out—as indeed they were, even sooner than expected. For in 1946, the General Assembly established the Committee on Information from Non-Self-Governing Territories. It was estab-

---

* Benson, "The International Machinery for Colonial Liberation," in Arthur Creech Jones (ed), *New Fabian Colonial Essays* (New York: Frederick A. Praeger, 1959), p. 228.

lished, however, against great opposition; but however maligned by the Belgians, Portuguese, and Spanish (although Spain is now supporting the Committee), however opposed by the colonial powers in general, this committee has continued ever since to exact from the administering authorities the statistics required by Article 73(e).

It was not simply the enforcement of regulations that made the Committee's work effective and fruitful; rather, it was by means of its persuasion, prodding, and criticism that it kept the colonial question alive and continually pricked the consciences of the colonial powers like Great Britain and France. As a result, the first decade of its life saw the number of non-self-governing territories fall from seventy-four to fifty-five, as such former territories as the Gold Coast and Malaya became independent, and the aggregate of their populations from about 215 million to just over 110 million. And by the end of 1956, Africa contained some 96 million dependent peoples out of a total population of 230 million. It is pertinent to mention, too, that my election to the Chairmanship of the Eleventh Session of the Committee on Information, in February, 1960, was greatly encouraging to the dependent peoples in Africa, for now the Committee was presided over by a representative of a country that itself had been, until March, 1957, a non-self-governing territory.

In reporting on the work of this Committee for the *United Nations Review* of May, 1960, I wrote the following comments:

> We are no longer dealing (as some people felt at San Francisco that they were) with a semipermanent state of affairs in which millions of people in Africa, Asia, the Pacific, and the Caribbean have to resign themselves to an indefinite period of tutelage exercised by other countries. The time of colonialism, benevolent or otherwise, is at last really running out.
>
> In my view, therefore, the General Assembly and the Committee on Information will need to give thought to revising their procedures, methods, and specific aims within the broad framework of

Chapter XI of the Charter, in order to function from now onward on the assumption that the non-self-governing territories will become independent sooner rather than later. The United Nations must find ways and means to bring all their influence and assistance to bear on the key problems which tend to delay or otherwise interfere with that process and which threaten to weaken independence once it has been attained. This calls for greater concentration on specific problems in certain territories: the problem of race relations, for example, in the East and Central African territories, where this is, in fact, the key to the evolution of democratic states; the problem of strong trade-union development in territories where indigenous labor forces are growing in size but are at a disadvantage in dealing with nonindigenous management; and the problem—an urgent one almost everywhere—of training local persons for the civil services and for the statutory bodies which are coming to play an increasingly important role in the economic and social advancement of most of these territories.

Were it not for such reports as these, which needled the colonial powers, encouraged debate between their representatives and those from Africa and Asia, and focused world attention on the colonial situation, the colonial powers might well have had their own way in the colonies. Simple statistics, therefore, proved valuable in the fight for African freedom and representation in the United Nations; and although political considerations were excluded from Article 73(e), the very fact that comparisons could be made from year to year on the pace of development in economic, social, and educational spheres had great political significance. For although political progress was not openly referred to in the Committee itself, it was inherent in every statistic discussed, and it rang as an obvious but unspoken question in the ears of the representatives of the colonial powers.

During the first ten years or so of the young United Nations' life, Africa spoke through the European powers and individual petitioners. At San Francisco in 1945, there were only three

African states that had achieved independence and were counted among the United Nations—Egypt (now the United Arab Republic), Ethiopia, and Liberia. But because each of them pursued policies consistent with her allies among the great powers, they could not act in concert. Moreover, Egypt then behaved as if she were not part of Africa because of her ties with the Arabian states across the Red Sea (Egypt has now recognized her full responsibilities in Africa, however), and the other two African states, although admitted to the world community, were not fully accepted. Yet, by the end of that first decade, there had taken place a tremendous transformation in Africa, the dimensions of which can be measured by the fact that there were soon to be thirty-two independent African states—an increase of twenty-nine in less than two decades. And still to come are such states as Kenya, Nyasaland, Northern and Southern Rhodesia, Angola, Mozambique, Bechuanaland, South-West Africa, Swaziland, Basutoland, and Cabinda. Such a transformation will continue to make it ludicrous for any nation outside Africa to ignore African opinion in matters that concern her directly.

Yet that great transformation cannot be measured simply in numbers, for the forces at work have been various—as various as the growing number of men and women, African and non-African, who began to work, together and apart, for the single purpose of achieving independence and freedom. Petitioners spoke and were questioned; visiting missions traveled back and forth between Africa and the United Nations; books and articles on Africa began to appear with increasing regularity; new ideas emerged, new convictions were born—and a new psychology began to evolve. It began to be viewed as inevitable that "sometime" the African territories would win their freedom, and both African sympathizers and African nationalists, sensing the change, began to redouble their efforts. All over the world, movements and organizations—for example, the American Committee on Africa, which planned conferences and circulated petitions on African questions—began to spring up, and, in turn, the forces of colonialism retaliated. Such an attempt was made, for example, by the British representative to the Trusteeship Council, Sir Alan Burns, who had been Governor of the Gold Coast during 1941–47 and, after his retirement from the United Nations, published a book (in 1957) entitled *In Defense of Colonies*. Striking back at the critics of British colonial policies who had goaded him during his years at the United Nations, he wrote:

> From Soviet Russia and her satellites comes the accusation that we exploit our colonies and deprive colonial peoples not only of the wealth that should belong to them, but also of that democratic self-government which is so dear to Communist authorities. From India, where the untouchables are still untouchable, come complaints of our racial discrimination. From Latin American countries, where two-thirds of the Amerindian populations are illiterate, we are reproached for the insufficient education given to the inhabitants of British colonial territories. From the United States, which calls its own colonies "possessions," there comes the denunciation of "colonialism." Even in this country, there is, in some quarters, a belief that our colonial empire is something to be ashamed of.[*]

It was a sign of the approaching end.

Yet the battle was not, in fact, being won by the anticolonial critics at the United Nations, however much they may have annoyed or harassed the representatives of the colonial powers. It was being won, instead, by the peoples of Asia who had proved they could win when they challenged the colonial powers, and by the peoples of Africa who were clearly readying themselves to make similar sacrifices in the cause of independence. In North Africa, for example, Morocco's success in the struggle with France for independence, achieved on March 3, 1956, was followed by Tunisia's independence on March 20, 1956. The Al-

[*] Burns, *In Defense of Colonies* (New York: The Macmillan Co., 1957), p. 13.

gerian war had begun on November 1, 1954, and it was to last for nearly eight years, offering proof, if proof were needed, that there were better ways to deal with colonial issues than to dispatch NATO troops to Africa. The Algerian uprising was followed by Dien Bien Phu, where the French lost their hold in the former Indochina. Then came the Bandung Conference of 1955. The French and the British could not but grow anxious at the prospect of waging long-drawn-out and costly wars in Africa under tropical conditions, particularly since the final result, in any case, might well prove to be, as the Asian experience had, independence for the colonial peoples. The conclusions they drew, as reflected in the French *loi-cadre* (that is, the basic law or constitution of the French Community) and in the independence of the Gold Coast in 1957, are now obvious; but had Africa's leaders shown the least timidity or hesitancy, had they shown themselves unwilling to face prison and even death for their convictions, the conclusions might have been quite different. Had Kwame Nkrumah not proved that he was ready to make every sacrifice, including that of going to jail in 1950, for the freedom of his country, the history of Ghana, and of Africa, might well have been different.

Although neither Mr. Macmillan nor I can say exactly when the "wind of change" began to blow, I think he might agree with me that it was in evidence during the events that led to the independence of Ghana in 1957 and that it has intensified every year since then. As the first British colonial territory in Africa to gain her independence, Ghana was in a unique position to lead the way toward the complete liberation of the African continent, and it was for these reasons that Osagyefo Dr. Nkrumah called for a conference of independent African states after he had consulted with other leaders in Africa. Thus, when the Accra Conference opened, it was an event of the greatest significance for many reasons—not the least of which was that it convened, as observers have since noted, to reverse the decisions made at the Congress of Berlin. The European powers had met in 1885 to dismember Africa; the African states in 1958 to unify Africa.

It was thus from the year 1958—the same year in which the first French-speaking state, Guinea, gained its independence—that we could begin to speak of a coherent group of independent African states working together, discussing mutual problems together, and encouraging African unity in all spheres of endeavor. It was at the Accra Conference that the delegates first agreed upon the need for further consultation and cooperation, decided upon their respective representatives at the United Nations as the best means of so doing, and, in effect, created an informal but permanent machinery of African states at the United Nations—referred to as the African Group.

As a result of the establishment of the African Group, a new era began both for the African states and for the United Nations itself. The African states have come to make important contributions on all United Nations problems and to take the lead in suggesting solutions to those problems which particularly affect Africa. The most urgent of these, surely, has been the future of dependent territories; since Africa is the only continent left where colonialism still holds sway, all African states are vitally concerned and do not hesitate, at the United Nations, to speak their minds. So forcefully do they speak, however, that some people have gained the impression of our African representatives as avengers, swooping down, sword in hand, upon the West, impervious to the voice of reason and dedicated only to revenging the injustices of the past. But this view of Africa is false; as Dr. Nkrumah said in his speech before the General Assembly in 1960: "Africa does not seek vengeance. It is against her very nature to harbor malice." The Africans are determined only to rid Africa of all vestiges of oppression, to make it unconditionally free, and thereby to allow the African Personality fully to realize itself. To that end, her representatives will speak out forcefully, and in unison, for the cause of independence.

Such unity was clearly demonstrated during the preparation and passing of the Declaration of Independence to colonial peoples and territories, which was adopted by the Fifteenth Session of the General Assembly, in December, 1960. It was reaffirmed at the Sixteenth Session, in September, 1961, when a follow-up resolution set up and charged a Committee of Seventeen with the task of overseeing the implementation of the Declaration. And it was readily apparent, during both sessions, in the preparation of resolutions calling for sanctions against the Republic of South Africa for its inhuman policy of apartheid.

The Declaration of 1960, which is contained in the General Assembly Resolution 1514(XV), made it clear that the subjection of peoples to alien forces is in itself a denial of fundamental human rights and therefore contrary to the Charter of the United Nations; that all peoples have a right to self-determination; and that it is pointless to argue the inadequacy of educational, economic, or political preparedness in order to delay independence. That is the essence of the Declaration, of which Paragraph 5 is so vital that it should be quoted:

> Immediate steps shall be taken in trust and non-self-governing territories or all other territories which have not yet attained independence, to transfer all powers to the peoples of those territories, without any conditions or reservations, in accordance with their freely expressed will and desire without distinction as to race, creed, or color, in order to enable them to enjoy complete independence and freedom.

There is no doubt in my mind that this Declaration is as important to Africa as the Charter of the United Nations and the Universal Declaration of Human Rights. It redresses an ancient injustice done to Africa; for if, indeed, Africa was the forgotten continent when the Charter was promulgated in 1946, the Declaration of 1960, calling for an immediate end to colonial rule in all territories, made it quite clear that Africa had taken her rightful place, and was expected to do so, in the United Nations.

Among other things, what had prompted the Declaration of 1960 was the so-called "Sharpeville incident." During the early part of 1960, the Pan-Africanist Congress of South Africa, a well organized African political party, had called on Africans to refuse to carry the iniquitous "pass cards" which every African is required by the South African Government to carry about on his person in order that his identity and movements can be instantly checked. In March, 1960, thousands of Africans openly burned their passes at Sharpeville, and it was during this orderly demonstration that the South African police, without provocation, fired on the unarmed Africans, wounding and killing many of them. Of course, the civilized world was shocked by the outrage; the Afro-Asian group at the United Nations immediately requested a meeting of the Security Council to consider the situation, which, in the opinion of the African states, threatened international peace and security. Thus, as a result of the Sharpeville incident of March 21, 1960, the Security Council of the United Nations passed a resolution that, among other things, called upon South Africa "to initiate measures aimed at bringing about racial harmony and equality in order to ensure that the present situation of apartheid does not continue to recur, and to abandon its policies of apartheid and racial discrimination."

It should be emphasized that South Africa's policy of apartheid is one of the most serious problems with which the United Nations is faced, and all independent African states are unified in their determination to solve it with every means at their disposal. At the Accra Conference, the delegates called upon all members of the United Nations "to intensify their efforts to combat and eradicate this degrading form of injustice," for all African states reject, without reservation, the practice of racial discrimination in whatever forms it may take. And because all attempts to persuade the South African Government to abandon its policy of apartheid have failed, the African states were again unanimous not only in condemning the policy but in recommending the imposition of sanctions by all nations. A number of African states, including Ghana, Sierra Leone, Ethiopia, Sudan, and Tanganyika, have already imposed sanctions against South Africa, but draft resolutions recommending sanctions by the United Nations had to be withdrawn in 1961 at the last moment because they lacked a two-thirds majority in the General Assembly. However, at the Seventeenth Session, in 1962, the General Assembly passed by an overwhelming majority a resolution calling for sanctions against South Africa.

There are complexities about the South African situation—notably involving the question of South-West Africa—that make it difficult to disentangle one issue from another. South-West Africa had been under German domination until World War I; as a result of Germany's defeat, it then became a mandate of the League of Nations, administered by the Union of South Africa; but after World War II, South Africa refused—and it was the only administering authority that did so—to enter into an international trusteeship agreement with the United Nations. Such a blatant refusal was, of course, morally reprehensible, and the great powers should, I think, have exercised their responsible authority to compel South Africa either to sign the trusteeship agreement or to surrender its administrative control to the United Kingdom. But in 1945, apparently, no one cared much about Africa and her peoples.

There suddenly appeared before the United Nations, however, to plead South-West Africa's case, an outstanding advocate of humanitarianism. The Reverend Michael Scott, a gaunt and intense Anglican clergyman thirsting for justice, first aroused the conscience of the world about the appalling situation that existed in the territory of South-West Africa. Seeming to burn with an apocalyptic flame, he warmed the hearts of the anticolonialist forces and singed the beards of the South Africans as he projected an intensely personal vision of a world that was not yet, but soon was to be, into the consciousness of busy delegates, cynical officials and blasé newsmen. It was as if a visionary, staring at some invisible object in the air, had suddenly walked into the councils of the world; the councilors themselves, unable to do more than glimpse what he so steadily saw before him, began to discuss among themselves just what he might be gazing at. Although his vision was dismissed by many as utopian, admirable but impracticable or unrealistic, he did set the delegates thinking; in some indefinable way, he began to change the situation, and he made a notable contribution to African freedom and independence.

Specifically, the Reverend Scott was concerned with the future of the Herero peoples, the dominant linguistic group in South-West Africa; beyond that, he was concerned with the injustice of apartheid in South Africa; and above all, he was interested in the peace of the world. He had read the Universal Declaration of Human Rights, promulgated in 1948, and had decided that it should also apply to the Herero peoples, with whose plight he had intimately associated himself. He was appointed the representative of the Herero peoples, having previously served prison terms in South Africa for opposing unjust racial laws, and in this capacity he became the first individual permitted to address the Trusteeship Committee (usually known as the Fourth Committee) of the General Assembly of the United Nations.

Nor has he ceased his efforts. He has returned year after year, up to the present time, as both petitioner and lobbyist, to appear before the Fourth Committee and the Committee on South-West Africa. Each time he has reappeared—he has had the assistance of colleagues on the Africa Defense Fund in London—he has called for action by the United Nations on South-West Africa. And he has called for action not on the grounds that it is expedient or practical, but on the grounds that South-West Africa was originally defeated with the aid of his own native country, Britain, which, over the years, has tended to defend South Africa in a vain attempt to keep it within the British Commonwealth. Although his most devoted supporters have finally conceded that, however magnificent, his struggle is in vain and that he will, in the end, die of a broken heart, he has continued to act according to his convictions. There finally came a day, in 1959, when South-West Africans themselves were able to send representatives of their own—men like the indefatigable Jariretundu Kozonguizi and the able, energetic, and intelligent Mburumba Kerina, a graduate of Lincoln University and now the New York representative of the South-West African People's Organization. These are only two who have taken up the burden that Scott has for so long been carrying. In the end, it will be the hearts of the supporters of apartheid that are broken, not the heart of the Reverend Michael Scott.

He has not, however, really been alone. For there have been countless battles waged before the Fourth Committee, as I have indicated, by individual petitioners, and each petition has made the delegates that much more aware of Africa and her problems. There have been countless debates and discussions in the United Nations itself, and there have been innumerable conferences among the Africans themselves. At the Addis Ababa Conference in 1960, for example, the delegates decided that the case of South-West Africa should be taken to the International Court of Justice for compulsory jurisdiction on the question of whether or not there had been a breach of the principles and purposes of the mandate. With the full support of all independent African states, the Empire of Ethiopia and the Republic of Liberia, as members of the defunct League of Nations, argued that the United Nations was the proper supervisory organ to which annual reports and petitions should be submitted by South Africa, that the United Nations' consent was a legal prerequisite and condition precedent to modification of the terms of the mandate, and that the South African Government had violated, and was violating, Article 22 of the Covenant of the League of Nations, Subsection 1 of which provides that:

> To those colonies and territories which are inhabited by peoples not yet able to stand by themselves under the strenuous conditions of the modern world, there should be applied the principle that the well-being and development of such peoples form a sacred trust of civilization and that securities for the performance of this trust should be embodied in this Covenant.

All the African states also agree, and we are supported by enlightened world opinion, that the South African policy of apartheid and the forcible removal of African families from one so-called "location" to another (a location is an artificial quarter of a town reserved for Africans by the South African administration) are completely at variance with certain articles of the mandate. For example, Article 2 says that "the mandatory shall promote to the utmost the material and moral well-being and the social progress of the inhabitants of the territory subject to the present mandate." Article 3 decrees: "The mandatory shall see that no forced labor is permitted, except for essential public works and services, and then only for adequate remuneration." And Article 4 prohibits the establishment of military and naval bases or the erection of fortifications in the territory. From these examples, it is evident that South Africa has definitely abused the sacred trust she assumed under the mandate and has treated South-West Africa as an integral part of South Africa. In my opinion, the African states should continue to seek for a solution to this complex issue on both legal and political levels. The International Court began deliberations on the question in October, 1962; but in the meantime the African states must continue to mobilize support both in Africa and at the United Nations. To that end, the unity of the independent African states in supporting resolutions on the South African situation has been most gratifying. At both the Fifteenth and Sixteenth Sessions of the General Assembly, for instance, the African delegates supported resolutions that deplored the actions of South Africa in refusing to cooperate with the United Nations on South-West Africa and in attempting to alter the status of that territory through a "referendum."

There are other powers, notably Great Britain, with a responsibility in the issues posed by South Africa and South-West Africa. Even if it can be argued—and I think it would be extremely difficult—that the League of Nations can be absolved from the responsibility and guilt of allowing an obviously racist government like South Africa to administer South-West Africa, Great Britain cannot so easily be absolved. Yet, even if it were possible so to argue, it is difficult to explain why Great Britain, as well as the other "High Contracting and Allied Powers," did not repair the "mistake" in 1945; and it is impossible to understand why the United Kingdom has done so little since 1961, when South Africa finally decided to leave the British Commonwealth rather than renounce her policy of apartheid. Today, when South Africa is shamelessly and openly governing the territory of South-West Africa on the basis of apartheid, a policy that has been condemned by the civilized world as inhuman, the United Kingdom should join with the independent states of Africa to rescue South-West Africa—at least to give it back to the United Nations, so to speak, so that the peoples of South-West Africa might be enabled to gain their independence. After all, South-West Africa was in the same position juridically as the Cameroons and Tanganyika, all three of which were, successively, German colonies and mandated territories; therefore, there is no good reason why the United Nations, including Great Britain and other major powers, should not exercise their full responsibilities in these matters.

Yet, even as late as 1962, the great powers seemed to have difficulty, despite their professed liberalism, in taking liberal positions on Africa. Eighty-six delegations present and voting supported a resolution of the Afro-Asian countries that set up a special committee of seven members to proceed to the territory of South-West Africa by May 1, 1962, for the following purposes:

1. To arrange for the evacuation of all South African troops from South-West Africa.
2. To arrange and supervise general elections to the Legislative Assembly of South-West Africa on the basis of universal adult suffrage.
3. To secure the repeal of all laws based on the policy of apartheid and racial discrimination.
4. To arrange for the free movement of the inhabitants, without confinement, to reserves or locations.
5. To arrange for the return to South-West Africa of all South-West African political leaders and freedom fighters now residing abroad.
6. To effect the release of all South-West African political prisoners.
7. To give assistance to the government that would be set up as a result of the general elections envisaged.

It was perhaps to be expected, in view of the atrocities committed by Portugal in Angola, that she would support South Africa on this issue by voting against it. But what is utterly beyond my ability to comprehend is the reason for the abstentions by the United Kingdom and France. Such abstentions, it appears to me, can be interpreted only as passive resistance to attempts to redress injustices in Africa, and they seem to provide a kind of reluctant assent, as well, to the South African Government's subsequent refusal to cooperate with the Committee of Seven. My colleagues and I, however, remain confident that the United Nations will soon resolve the South-West African issue and so vindicate the work of petitioners like the Reverend Michael Scott who have dedicated themselves to restoring to the peoples of South-West Africa equality, dignity, and independence.

In addition to the Congo, already discussed in an earlier chapter, and South-West Africa, there have been a number of other specific problems before the United Nation to which the independent African states have made valuable contributions. I shall take them up one by one in order to suggest not only the range of problems but the African attitudes toward them. The war in Algeria, for example, was regarded by the African states as an aspect of the larger question of the future of nonindependent territories in Africa, and it became a subject of constant discussion within the United Nations—largely through the initiative taken by African and Asian nations—for nearly five years. Every African conference, in addition, made pronouncements on the situation and decried the senseless war that for eight long years destroyed the youth of Algeria and France. As a matter of fact, it was to further a resolution passed at the Accra Conference of 1958—which called upon France "to enter into negotiations with the Provisional Government of Algeria with a view to reaching a final and just settlement"—that the African ambassadors to the United Nations staged their most spectacular campaign of collective lobbying. Not only did they lobby as usual among the missions accredited to the United Nations, but they organized selected teams of diplomats from their missions to visit the Latin American and Scandinavian counries in order to plead the cause of Algerian independence and request support—or, at least, abstention—at the next session of the General Assembly.

These efforts were highly successful. During the Thirteenth Session of the General Assembly, in 1958, a resolution favoring Algerian independence and calling for negotiations failed by only a single vote to gain the required two-thirds majority. At the next session, the Fourteenth, the African states, in cooperation with twenty-two Asian states, again tried and failed; but since General de Gaulle had just offered self-determination to the Algerian people, most delegations then considered it the wiser choice to await the outcome of his offer. At the Fifteenth Session, however, there was a resolution passed by the United Nations—a resolution that "recognizes the imperative need for adequate and effective guarantees to assure the successful and just implementation of the right of self-determination on the basis of respect for unity and territorial integrity of Algeria" and "recognizes further that the United Nations has a responsibility to contribute toward its successful and just implementation." On this resolution, however, the independent African states were divided; several of the former French African colonies, for reasons already noted, took a sympathetic attitude toward France.

To the African delegations and to all who supported the resolution, it was gratifying indeed that France and the Algerian Provisional Government were able to meet at Evian-les-Bains, on May 18, 1961, to begin serious negotiations. Although the negotiations were broken off all too soon in a disagreement about the exploitation of the Sahara resources, the African states spared no efforts within and outside the United Nations to secure a resumption of negotiations. It has, of course, been in the interest of Africa that the war should cease and that Algeria should become an independent nation within the United Nations. But although General de Gaulle has understood, better than any other French statesman, the temper of Africa, he has been impeded in his efforts by right-wing politicians in France and a million European settlers in Algeria. The behavior of the latter, the *colons,* has been like that of other white minority groups in Africa, whether in South Africa, Angola, or the Congo's Katanga Province: They are always eager and happy to dominate the indigenous Africans, the majority, but as soon as the African

Personality begins to reassert itself, they become fearful of African rule—a completely inexplicable attitude, since it runs counter to the equality, freedom, and dignity for which the African Personality stands. At any rate, they will have an opportunity to prove to themselves how baseless their fears really are: On July 1, 1962, after a referendum in which the people voted in favor of independence and cooperation with France, Algeria became an independent nation.

Another matter of great concern to the African states has been that of nuclear testing, already referred to from time to time in other contexts. I mention it here, however—particularly the specific problem of French testing in the Sahara—to suggest again how contradictory or inconsistent the great powers can be in their attitudes toward, and their treatment of, Africa. From the time of the Accra Conference, the independent African states had declared themselves against the production of nuclear and thermonuclear weapons; but when it became known that the French were preparing to explode a nuclear device in the Sahara, the independent African states met specifically to discuss the problem at Monrovia, Liberia, in August, 1959. A resolution was then passed "denouncing vigorously and with profound indignation the decision of any government to carry out nuclear tests in the Sahara or in any part of Africa." Subsequently—and primarily because of Afro-Asian efforts—a General Assembly resolution was passed by a two-thirds majority requesting France "to refrain from conducting such tests in the Sahara." France not only flouted the resolution, but conducted four tests on African soil—a flagrant violation that the independent African states, among others, will remember, since France had no rights whatsoever to conduct its tests on African soil. A General Assembly resolution, however, has since made it highly improbable that France or any other power will try any more nuclear experiments in Africa, for the resolution declares Africa a denuclearized zone, as President Nkrumah proposed in the General Assembly in September, 1960.

Still another matter of major concern to Africa has been the problem of economic development. Since all African states are economically underdeveloped, they face common problems—the lack of capital, the shortage of managerial and technical skills, the need for economic diversification, and the difficulties of providing a higher standard of living for their peoples. In short, they are confronted with the proverbial vicious circle: They are poor because they have no capital; they have no capital because they have no savings; and they have no savings because they are poor. All African states, therefore, must find the means either at home or abroad to break this circle, and it is clear that they intend to do so. Although each African nation still retains the sovereign right to enter into bilateral financial agreements with more advanced countries in order to secure the necessary foundations for further development, all are firm in their resolve to develop Africa as an economic unit by means of regional organizations for economic cooperation. Such organizations will formulate plans for the establishment of an African development bank, an African common market, an African airways, and other systems of use and benefit to the whole continent. And that is where the United Nations and its specialized agencies enter the picture.

During the Sixteenth Session of the General Assembly, the African delegations succeeded in persuading the Assembly to pass a resolution that urged "the importance of establishing regional economic development banks for Africa . . . and requests the Secretary-General to consult with the appropriate institutions, particularly the International Bank for Reconstruction and Development, on the immediate steps necessary for the early establishment of these regional development banks." However, since Ghana, Nigeria, Sierra Leone, and Tanganyika are in the sterling area, Liberia uses the dollar, and the former French colonies use francs, it has been necessary, as a start, to adapt the regional bank to the existing economic and financial structures of various African regions. It may well turn out, however, that one central development bank in control of the regional branches will prove the most expeditious means of coping with economic development. What must be avoided, at any rate, is the duplication of effort that leads to expensive waste, for there is an urgent need in Africa to employ every available resource for the betterment of the continent as a whole.

Again, largely through the efforts of the African states, the General Assembly appointed a committee to examine the possibility of setting up a capital development fund. However, the donor countries—the United States, the Union of Soviet Socialist Republics, the United Kingdom, Czechoslovakia, and others —oppose such a step on the grounds that the International Bank for Reconstruction and Development already serves the purpose of helping underdeveloped countries. What they fail to mention in their arguments is that the World Bank tends to be parsimonious; it does not lend money without the fulfillment of rigorous conditions—for example, that the project for which a loan is requested be demonstrably feasible—and it does not do so, even then, without protracted negotiations. What is envisaged under the capital development fund of the United Nations, however, is an organization wih readily available financial resources from which needy countries, in Africa and elsewhere, can borrow at low rates of interest. Such a system, if they could only realize it, might serve the enlightened self-interests of the donor countries; but in the present Cold War between East and West, the major powers prefer the clarity of bilateral agreements, by which they can make friends, allies, or even dependents, to the obscurity of multilateral forms of investment, which tend to diminish the struggle dividing the world into two opposing camps.

There have been a number of achievements in other fields. Specialized agencies of the United Nations—the Food and Agricultural Organization, the World Health Organization, the United Nations Educational, Scientific, and Cultural Organization, the International Labour Office—have been helping African governments upon request. The regular and expanded programs of technical assistance have also found great favor in Africa and redounded to the credit of the United Nations. Some $7.5 million was spent in Africa for technical assistance between 1958 and 1960; under the expanded program, Africa (excluding the U.A.R.) has received $23 million betwen 1960 and 1961; and pre-investment activities envisaged under the Special Fund have added some $18 million to date. This spirit of international cooperation has convinced African nations of the need for more such United Nations technical-assistance operations in Africa—provided only that the experience of the Congo (Léopoldville) is avoided. The political crisis brought quite a few experts and a great deal of money into the Congo. During July, 1961, for example, the United Nations spent about $300,000 for technical assistance and sent 405 experts in all fields, and during 1962 it has spent about $10 million a month there for the entire operation. But although a great deal has been accomplished through such economic and technical assistance to salvage the economy of the new republic, the political crisis and the resulting chaos allowed for too much political interference, both covert and overt, on the part of the experts, the magnitude of which cannot be described here. Suffice it to say that all African states, with the exception of one or two like Congo (Brazzaville), whose heads of state sided with Moise Tshombe of Katanga, support fully the actions taken by U Thant, Acting Secretary-General of the United Nations, to end forever the stranglehold upon Katanga by powerful European financiers.

Although I have been speaking of the African Group at the United Nations, I do not wish to leave the impression that the independent African states represent a bloc. If they have spoken with one voice on many occasions, the reason is that they believe so passionately in the principles of self-determination and independence for all peoples, and of peaceful coexistence among the peoples of the world. Yet, on many questions, especially non-African questions, there are differences of opinion among the African states, largely because of differences in foreign policies. I have briefly discussed some of these, such as the Cold War issues of Hungary, Cuba, and the reorganization of the U.N. Secretariat. But there are others, such as the admission to the United Nations of the People's Republic of China, on which African states have voted both for and against. At the Sixteenth Session, in 1961, Ghana voted to seat the Peking Government, but Congo (Brazzaville), Gabon, and Ivory Coast joined France in voting against admission; Ghana, like the United Kingdom and other countries, has recognized the People's Republic of China, but France has not. In any case, Ghana believes that the United Nations is the proper forum for ironing out such differences in order to halt as quickly as possible any threat of war; for that reason, she believes that China must be represented so that she may assume her international obligations and responsibilities in the community of nations.

Such differences admittedly do exist, and they are healthy ones, for they promote debate and thought, argument and decision, action and progress. The common approach that the African Group has so far adopted on questions of war and peace, social and economic development, and fundamental human rights has been based upon the best interests of the entire African continent. Yet, as the African Group fully realizes, the best interests of the African continent are intimately involved with the United Nations, and every African state, including those yet to achieve independence, believes that the United Nations remains the best hope of mankind. The United Nations may not yet be a world government, and it may never be; for, as the late Secretary-General Dag Hammarskjöld said in 1957:

> The Charter read as a whole does not endow the United Nations with any of the attributes of a superstate or of a body active outside the framework of decisions of member governments. The United Nations is, rather, an instrument for negotiating among and, to some extent, for governments. It is also an instrument added to the time-honored means of diplomacy for concerting action by governments in support of the goals of the Charter. This is the role the organization has played, sometimes successfully, sometimes with disappointing setbacks, throughout its life.

Since Mr. Hammarskjöld's words still apply today, it is fitting that the United Nations should therefore continue to bear a close relationship to the facts of international life. Since the membership, for example, has increased from its original 55 members to 110, and since the great majority of new member nations come from Africa, it is reasonable to suggest that Africa should be proportionately represented in all the organs of the United Nations, including the Secretariat. To redress the present imbalance, I think, we must allocate, on the basis of equitable geographical distribution (a mode of representation already agreed upon by the United Nations), seats to Africa in both the Security Council and the Economic and Social Council. And since the principle has now been accepted of having at the top echelon of the Secretariat at least one Deputy Secretary-General or Under-secretary from Africa, I think the Secretariat should be so organized that there will be African officers at all levels.

I make these suggestions simply because Africa is fast rising to her full stature. A re-emergent Africa, in which and through which the African Personality is being realized, intends to play her full and responsible role in our world organization in order to make the United Nations an effective instrument for peace and progress and a forum where all the problems of the world may be debated and resolved for the benefit of all mankind. For it has only been since the admission of the independent states of Africa that the United Nations has truly begun to become a universal organization in the service of humanity. Africa has helped to make the United Nations more truly itself.

VI

Reflections of a Young Statesman

What is the use of living if it be not to strive for noble causes and to make this muddled world a better place for those who will live in it after we are gone? How else can we put ourselves in harmonious relation with the verities and consolations of the infinite and the external? I avow my faith that we are marching toward better days. Humanity will not be cast down. We are going on, swinging bravely forward along the grand high road, and already behind the distant mountains is the promise of the sun.

So WINSTON CHURCHILL wrote in *Faith in the Future,* and his belief in better days to come is one that I, and most Africans, share. In this small undertaking of mine, I have concentrated largely on Africa's attempts to assert her personality and so "unbind" herself from foreign domination and the threat of strangulation. I have done so in order to correct the image of Africa so long fixed in the minds of those non-Africans who still regard Africa as a continent inhabited by peoples with no personalities of their own. For it is obvious that the Africa that should have been—indeed, the Africa that would have been had not colonialism gained control of the continent—can only come into being, can only realize itself during the latter half of the twentieth century if tremendous efforts are made to bridge the gap of centuries of exploitation and neglect. Those who have faith in Africa, the

Africans, will do their share, will give their all, as they have been doing for so long now; but their work will be made a great deal easier if the non-Africans will grant them—and surely it is not too much to ask of other human beings—the dignity, respect, and equality we all need to survive. If the African is regaining his faith in the future, surely the non-African can, too; and if both are working together, within the framework of African unity, those efforts will be fruitful indeed.

I believe in African unity. Today, in Africa, there is the unity of deprivation, of underdevelopment, since there is not a single country that is industrialized. Tomorrow, there must be the unity of growth, of development, and it can be achieved only by the united efforts of all African nations. Today, almost every African state possesses an economy with an agricultural sector of over 90 per cent, as compared to the 20–30 per cent devoted to the agricultural sector in Europe and America. Yet, in every African state, that economy is a colonial economy that still relies heavily on a single exportable product such as cocoa, cotton, groundnuts, bananas, or copper. And in every African state, the average per capita national income is no more than $250 annually. The following statistics provide a graphic indication of the desperate need for economic development:

Country	Population	Annual per capita national income
Congo (Léopoldville)	14 million	$ 90
Gabon	420,000	$100
Ghana	7 million	$171
Guinea	3 million	$ 52
Ethiopia	22 million	$ 45
Liberia	2.5 million	$124
Ivory Coast	3.5 million	$100
Mali	4.5 million	$ 51
Nigeria	35 million	$ 79

Such is the present level of income—despite the enormous wealth Africa has at its command. True the natural resources are not equitably distributed throughout Africa, and the result is, of course, that some countries are richer than others in both human and material resources. But all are striving to improve their economic and social positions; and since all lack sufficient capital, technical skills, and personnel (as well as both managerial and executive leaders), all African governments must do the best they can to improvise and yet to lay secure foundations. Ghana, for example, began with a development plan that concentrated upon providing the basic infrastructure upon which a more developed economy could, in time, be built: more and better roads, improved water supplies and electric power, and modernized communication and transportation facilities. As these were being developed, educational opportunities, particularly those emphasizing managerial and technical training, were being expanded. By now, Ghana spends $42 million annually on education, as compared to some $18 million before independence, and it has added 20 more training colleges for teachers and two new universities. The same efforts are also being made in other African countries, particularly in Nigeria, where a very large proportion of the federal revenue is being devoted to education and to the diversification of the economy.

The danger, however, in such individual, hence necessarily divided, efforts by African states to build up their parts of the continent is that of slowing down the development of the continent as a whole. Since immediate needs are always so pressing, the general good, which seems so far distant and is so difficult to achieve, is often sacrificed; but there is everything to gain, as African leaders like Emperor Haile Selassie of Ethiopia and President Kwame Nkrumah of Ghana keep insisting, if Africa can be developed as an economic unit. This kind of African unity ranges from concerted efforts to do away with bribery, corruption, feudal privileges, and the growth of *nouveau riche* classes to a judicious economic and social plan of development that will improve the standards of living of all by concentrating on such basic issues as the right of everyone, regardless of birth, to good shelter, nutritious food, education, and the chance to prove himself a hero or a knave. Africa cannot, I think, afford the luxury of unbridled capitalism and its attendant evils, nor do I think it wishes to. Some observers, like Peter Ritner, author of *The Death of Africa*,* argue that the individual African states are engaged in cutthroat competition for foreign capital and that Africa is doomed to die in the process. The latter is an assumption I cannot at all agree with, for reasons that will be obvious to anyone who has followed my arguments thus far. Admittedly, there will be an intensive quest for finance capital and for technical assistance for economic development, but the willingness and enthusiasm among the African peoples themselves to develop their countries and their continent can lead only to growth and maturity, not to decay and death. Mr. Ritner seems to have an erroneous understanding of the temper and spirit of an Africa unbound, for Africa is very much alive, eager to harness her energies as other free areas have, and she will grow from strength to strength to emerge in a union embracing the whole continent.

For my part, I am convinced that a West African federation of states is possible even tomorrow. Ever since my student days at Oxford, I have shared this conviction with colleagues from Nigeria, Sierra Leone, Ghana, Gambia, and Senegal. If an East African federation like that outlined by Julius Nyerere of Tanganyika can come into being, too, such regional federations, including the Maghreb, will provide the steppingstones to a complete federation of the whole of Africa. My belief in the United States of Africa is perhaps surpassed only by that of Dr. Nkrumah, whose views I fully share in this matter. I agree with him that it is possible to achieve immediately a confederation of African states whose members will retain their national anthem, flag, and sovereignty, but will surrender political control in matters concerning economic development, defense, and foreign policy. Such

* New York: The Macmillan Co., 1961.

a confederation may have a confederate parliament of two houses
—an upper house in which all African states are equally represented and a lower house in which representatives are selected
proportionately according to population; but it should function
only within the framework of powers granted it by the constituent
states, and my own conviction is that the emphasis should be
placed on social and economic reconstruction and on cultural
development, under adequate political direction.

It should not be forgotten, however, that the question of
African unity, particularly in the modern era, includes the considerations and interests not only of individual African nations
but the nations of the world as well. Everywhere today, man is
striving to achieve a better understanding of his fellow man;
but because of the rank discriminations, injustices, and atrocities
suffered by African slaves and their descendants in the Western
Hemisphere, there has been an enormous revolt against Europeans in Africa for over a century. In more recent years, as racial
understanding has improved, people of African descent have
nevertheless been struggling for recognition in the Caribbean
and the Americas as human beings capable of achievement. The
invocation of Negritude, for example, by such poets as Aimé
Césaire of Martinique and Léopold Senghor of Senegal can indeed be regarded, as I have pointed out, as part of this revolt.
The veteran Dr. W. E. B. Du Bois—an American with African
and French blood in his veins who now lives in Ghana, where
he is preparing an encyclopedia Africana—wrote in his book
The Negro:

> There is slowly arising not only a curiously strong brotherhood of
> Negro blood throughout the world, but the common cause of
> the darker races against the intolerable assumptions and insults of
> Europeans has already found expression. Most men in the world
> are colored. A belief in humanity means a belief in colored men.
> The future world will, in all reasonable possibility, be what colored
> men make it.

This, too, is part of the theory of Negritude. As practiced in Brazil, however, Negritude has led to the mixing of bloods until Aryan and Negro are completely mixed; it was, in fact, considered fashionable there some time ago to claim that one had Negro blood in his veins. Yet Negritude interpreted in this way is a dangerous creed: Why should the color of a man's skin mean anything? After all, race is less a biological than a social myth; what is truly important is the self-respect and mutual understanding among all human beings of whatever "color." That is why, for me, at least, the concept of the African Personality is much more appealing than Negritude; for whatever riches it may contribute to humankind, the African Personality does not seek for itself special privileges. All of us will, I think, agree that we must avoid a world like George Orwell's *Animal Farm,* in which some individuals become more equal than others; and the African idea, simply stated, is rather that of a world in which the human personality may flower fully in its various individual forms.

The concept of the African Personality embodies the humanity of the African—his courtesy, tolerance, ready smile, and warmth of friendship toward all peoples. Indeed, it is not too much to say that Europeans were tolerated in most parts of Africa precisely because of the African's courtesy and affection for other human beings. However, this affection was abused by the European empire-builders in numerous ways. At one time, for instance, British colonial officers, upon embarking for service in Africa, were given a booklet that offered hints and tips on dealing with Africans. In case of misunderstandings, disagreements, or other differences, the colonial officers were, according to the booklet, merely to show their teeth in a broad grin because it would surely make the African thaw. Such advice was, of course, a thorough misinterpretation of the African's personality, and such abuses were bound to undermine the foundations of faith and trust. Mutual self-respect is still the only possible basis for a satisfactory relationship, and the African Personality is it-

self an affirmation that such relationships are not only possible
but desirable and realizable.

Yet, if the search for African unity must take into account the
other nations of the world as well, it must also assess the influences that have, in the last century at least, been imposed upon
African culture. Such influences as Christian education, modern
science and technology (particularly, perhaps, medicine), and
European political and moral philosophy have, without doubt,
left their impression on African minds. But, as I have argued
earlier in this book, the normal processes of diffusion and contact
with the outside world—that is, had there been no colonial rule
in Africa—would have rendered African societies dynamic and
progressive in their own good time. But the enforced introduc-
tion of European ideas and philosophies has tended to stultify,
and therefore throw into confusion and turbulence, indigenous
African values, ideas, and aspirations for the development of
African social and political institutions. That is, of course,
one important reason for the African Personality's insistence
upon discovering—really rediscovering—what is essentially and
uniquely African about itself. For only in being truly African
can the African Personality be truly human.

It therefore follows, I think, that as Africa continues to evolve
its own personality, philosophy, and government, it cannot—indeed, it should not—become another Europe or America. Although it cannot help but be influenced by the colonial past,
and may indeed draw upon that past for whatever it may be able
to assimilate, Africa will be better off, more completely unbound,
if it sheds all unnecessary European trappings in order to concentrate upon the work of developing within the African mold
and within the international community to which it subscribes.
So when I am asked by outside observers whether or not I think
the independent African states can practice democracy and resist Communism, I say that I do not understand these terms. As
far as I am concerned, political institutions develop in the par-

ticular context, the particular circumstances and conditions of a given country or region, and I think it unrealistic to expect that an African nation will develop political institutions that are carbon copies of those—whether of England, Russia, China, or the United States—which have originated in different contexts and circumstances. No one has taught or really can teach democracy to the Africans, and it is fallacious to claim that the colonial powers have at least bequeathed a democratic form of government to the newly independent African states. The fact is, rather, that the process of democratizing governmental institutions under colonial regimes actually occurred because African nationalists insisted that they be given a voice in running their various governments. Although they were admittedly imbued with the revolutionary ideas of thinkers like Marx, Rousseau, Paine, Mill, and Machiavelli, the African nationalists, not the colonialists, demanded "One man, one vote; one vote, one value," for the colonial rulers were interested only in holding on to what they had for their own profit and amusement. I think it much wiser, therefore, to let the historians give a name to the results of the African search; but I will predict, from my own experience, that if we mean by socialism a form of communalism, then it is possible that such may be the verdict of history. For the ever-increasing desire of Africans to abolish poverty, disease, and ignorance and to reconstruct our countries both economically and socially can lead only to the eradication of avarice, exploitation, discrimination, and the inequities of class systems.

I have a firm belief in the United Nations. It is a fine and noble organization, where problems may be introduced, discussed, and resolved by representatives from nearly every country in the world. It serves as a great experiment in man's attempt to live peaceably with his fellow man, and its value and vitality may both be measured by the occasional attacks made upon it by individuals and nations. Despite these attacks, there have been many problems solved through the agency of the United Nations —the problem of Lebanon, for example, in 1958—and there have been still others in which the United Nations, although not itself responsible for resolving the disputes, has contributed by providing the world-wide forum in which the preliminary arguments, so necessary to a peaceful solution, could be presented. The abatement of the Cuban crisis of October, 1962, is an example.

Just settlements of disputes are not, in fact, suddenly discovered like a new planet in the firmament. Rather, they are reached through the long process of discussion and negotiation and a mutual willingness to give and to take. The process, however, cannot begin at all until both sides have shown a desire to reach an agreement in good faith, for the art of negotiation is a complex one, involving patience, poise, and understanding. But since the United Nations constitutes a family of nations in a very real sense, in which individual diplomats are exposed to the frank comments of their peers and to the critical gaze of public opinion throughout the world, it serves to place the problem under discussion in perspective, to take the edge off the sharpest disputes, and to encourage both delegate and disputant to review their positions within the framework of the world community as a whole. Whether it is a frontier dispute, an act of aggression, a threat of invasion, a question of finance, or an issue of human rights, the chances are good that a similar problem has come before the United Nations in the past and that it can, therefore, be treated in a variety of ways—not on the basis of what is said in the press, but on the basis of the collective judgment of the permanent representatives, their governments, and the members of the Secretariat. And the resolution that is eventually passed usually reflects neither the sharp and even passionate nationalistic overtones that might otherwise obscure the real issue under discussion nor the strength of the feelings of the opposing sides. The various influences at work in such situations, the individual or collective lobbying that does go on behind the scenes, are not easily noticeable or understandable to the uninitiated, but those of us who have been involved in the delicate art of multilateral negotiations fully realize and appreciate the tremendous force for peace that the United Nations wields in the world today.

I need say no more about the great changes that have occurred in international policies and human affairs since the Charter was signed at San Francisco in 1945. But it is disturbing to note that those who previously enjoyed privileged positions within the United Nations do not find it easy to adapt to the new and universal society that is now emerging. Both European and American diplomats have expressed a good deal of anxiety that the admission of such a large number of African states will lead to the domination of the United Nations by the Afro-Asian group, and there have even been dire predictions that the United Nations is about to collapse. Such attitudes are, indeed, unfortunate, for the Charter of the United Nations, signed by those very European and American nations, establishes the principle of the organization as one based on the sovereign equality of all its members and on the universality of membership. Although more than half of the 110 member nations—6 more were admitted during the Seventeenth Session of the General Assembly in 1962—are members of the Afro-Asian group, they have contributed a good deal of purposeful vitality that will benefit every nation in the world, and this fact hardly hints at the collapse of the United Nations. When, for instance, the British Foreign Secretary, Lord Home, asserted in December, 1961, that the United Nations was in danger of collapse because it was changing its purpose from an organization committed to keeping the peace to one concerned with liquidating colonialism, he completely missed the point that the liquidation of colonialism will in itself contribute greatly to the maintenance of peace in the world. Like many other European statesmen, he seems too genuinely European to adapt himself to ideas from Asia and Africa that are not in accord with traditionally accepted beliefs. There is no reason, to be sure, why the older nation-states should not, if they choose, cling to such attitudes and standards, but it is hardly fair for them to conclude that any departure from what they have come to accept and cherish in good faith is necessarily suspect or will lead to the end of the world. Universal standards there must be, and the very existence of the United Nations is a testimony to that conviction; but those universal standards must be evolved by all nations, and they can be evolved only by the agreement arrived at in the conflict of debate, in the acceptance of new ideas, and in the willingness to grant others the rights one expects for himself.

If, then, this were the situation, as indeed it promises to be, there might be no need for groups acting in their own interests. But it should not, given the history of colonialism, surprise anyone that a group like the Afro-Asians does, in some sense, exist; what may be surprising, however, is the restraint, responsibility, and dedication to peace with which the Afro-Asian group has acted. I have, myself, had the opportunity of working for more than three years in close cooperation with able and responsible ambassadors from the Afro-Asian world like U Thant of Burma, Chandra Jha of India, Diallo Telli of Guinea, Tesfaye Gebre-Egzy of Ethiopia, Omar Loutfi and Mahmoud Riad of the United Arab Republic, Omar Adeel of Sudan, Adnan Pachachi of Iraq, Malalasekera of Ceylon, Mongi Slim and Taieb Slim of Tunisia, Abdul Pazhwak of Afghanistan, Nathan Barnes of Liberia, Gershon Collier of Sierra Leone, and Assouan Usher of Ivory Coast—men who have shown great ability, tact, and experience in their activities at the United Nations. The declaration on colonialism, for example, which is embodied in Resolution 1514(XV), cannot be regarded by anyone as an irresponsible act of statesmanship. It simply asserts that the subjection of peoples to alien domination and exploitation is contrary to the Charter of the United Nations and is an impediment to peace and cooperation in the world, and it proclaims the necessity of bringing to a speedy and unconditional end colonialism in all its forms and manifestations. The late Secretary-General Dag Hammarskjöld wrote favorably about the implications of this resolution in his annual report presented before the Sixteenth Session of the General Assembly, and I think it must be said that the resolution reflects the most cohesive and coordinated action yet taken by the Afro-Asian nations in their own interest and for the peace of the world at large. Furthermore, a contribution of this sort, undertaken by a group of na·' tions from Asia and Africa, has the added advantage of making the United Nations itself more of a universally active organization. The increase in membership means not that the organization is losing sight of its peace-keeping role, but that all nations have active opportunities to play purposeful parts in world affairs. In the past, such opportunities were denied to Africa; but I think that once Europe—or at least the former colonial powers —can adapt to the recognition that it no longer controls the destinies of other areas of the world and that there is now a world community of nations in which each state has a rightful seat, then the United Nations will be able to play an even more meaningful role than has yet been possible.

It is widely recognized that fear of the Afro-Asian voting strength has led the great powers to pit state against state in an effort to offset that power. They have, for example, tried to divide the African Group by playing the so-called "extremist" and "moderate" factions against one another. Dangerous as it is to pin misleading labels upon whole groups of nations—merely adding to the confusion—I think it much more dangerous to attempt to thwart or subvert the collective will of the African nations at the United Nations, since such tactics not only create resentment among the peoples of Africa but clearly indicate that the great powers still wish to retain a measure of control, however indirectly, over the course of international events. The West-

ern powers have even dropped dark hints that they may withdraw
from the United Nations; the ostensible reason for such a threat
is that the Afro-Asian states have come to regard the United
Nations as their own organization, but the real reason seems
to be that the Western powers fear the loss of the dominant position they have so long held in the world organization. They evidently reason that if one or more of the Western powers should
withdraw, cutting off budget contributions at the same time, the
Afro-Asians would at once come to heel—would, in fact, be
forced to come to heel simply because small nations, like those in
Africa, need the United Nations more than the larger countries.
Fortunately, a number of Western nations, particularly the
Scandinavian countries, are becoming increasingly aware of
the effective and responsible role of the Afro-Asian group. In any
case, I do not believe for a minute that the Afro-Asian states
would have to capitulate, however much they may need the
United Nations; for, short of the world being blown up in an
atomic cataclysm, the United Nations will continue to survive.

I do not take the threat of withdrawal very seriously either,
for it has not, in the past, been helpful for any power to boycott
the United Nations. Neither Germany nor Italy found that its
withdrawal from the League of Nations advanced its national
interests in the long run, and I am sure that the Soviet Union
regrets the absence of its representatives from the United Nations
during the first fateful days of the Korean War in 1950. If the
Government of South Africa were to make a confession, I think
its leaders would have to admit that South Africa, not the United
Nations, suffered as a result of her withdrawal in 1955. In the
absence of her representatives, the tone of resolutions on South
Africa's apartheid policy grew stronger year by year; and since
her return to the fold, South Africa has had an unusually difficult time. That country is, of course, in a peculiar position, and
I really doubt that she will be comfortable or happy within the
international community until she has abolished her policies of

apartheid. Yet, however opposed I am to the policies of states like Portugal and South Africa, whose inhuman treatment of Africans has earned the opprobrium of all who believe in the Charter of the United Nations and the Covenant of Human Rights, I now believe (although I used to be one of those who advocated their expulsion from the United Nations) that Portugal and South Africa should be represented so that they may be exposed to world opinion and international pressure to change their colonial policies. The United Nations, I firmly believe, should be represented by all states big and small, poor and rich, perfect and imperfect—provided, of course, that they scrupulously observe its Charter and consider its decisions morally binding at the very least.

For such reasons as these, therefore, I find it difficult to understand why the great powers should be so fearful of the intentions of the Afro-Asian group. If I and my colleagues from the smaller nations of Africa are willing to hear other points of view and to grant nations whose policies we abhor admission to the United Nations, why should the great powers, larger and stronger than we, not do the same? Why should those larger nations stoop to tactics of subversion and threats of withdrawal—unless, of course, as I have suggested, they do so in order to impose their will, as they did in the past, on nations that once were their colonies? For them, however, as I can well understand, it must be difficult to adjust to a new universal society in which all nations have equal voices, but they should realize, too, how sensitive the Afro-Asian nations must be to any forms of coercion, no matter how disguised; and I think that the great powers would be better advised to change from tactics of subversion and threats of withdrawal to open and frank discussion. Surely, at this stage in the development of the world community that most men of good will obviously desire, it is not unreasonable to ask that we all bear in mind not only the principles and purposes but the spirit of the Charter of the United Nations.

My own faith in the United Nations was immeasurably strengthened by the late Dag Hammarskjöld. Whether or not his love for the United Nations grew from his tenure of office I do not, of course, know; but I do know that his faith in the world organization was enormous. To me, he was not only a great world figure but was fast becoming a symbol of the United Nations itself. I had the utmost respect for his courtesy, cultivation, wit, and intelligence. Although he made mistakes, I still stand by the tribute I paid him during the Security Council debate on the Congo, on August 9, 1960, when I was moved to quote the words used by Burke in 1774 in his tribute to the Earl of Chatham: "Sir, the venerable age of this man, his merited rank, his superior eloquence, his splendid qualities, his eminent services, the vast space he fills in the eyes of mankind will not suffer me to censure any part of his conduct." As I spoke those words, Hammarskjöld blushed, but he must have known that I recognized him as a very great man indeed. I am also convinced that he knew Ghana's policy toward the Congo was basically sound; unfortunately, however, he was a year too late in recognizing it— and then he died in the cause of the peace of the Congo, of Africa, and of the world.

Hammarskjöld was completely unprepared for the Congo situation. The crisis broke suddenly, he had to reorient himself, and, perhaps inevitably, he displayed some prejudices. For example, there was his prejudice against the late Patrice Lumumba; as a perusal of the correspondence exchanged between the two men during a fateful week in 1960 makes clear, Hammarskjöld failed to comprehend how an African could possibly aspire to cross swords with him. In the Congo, there was a struggle in process, one that would reverberate throughout Central and Southern Africa, where a minority of Europeans had pledged themselves to maintain white supremacy at all costs; in this struggle, Lumumba represented, as it were, the African Personality standing firm against all odds, and he did so with the staunch support of

African leaders like Nkrumah, Touré, Keita, Nasser, and the late King Mohammed of Morocco. But in the end Lumumba was sacrificed in order that the Congo might be united.

Since I was involved in the Congo crisis from the very beginning, I can say that I am proud of Ghana's approach and her stand. Our support for the Congo was based on the strategy not of acquiring an ally to offset Nigeria's size, as *The New York Times* and others implied, but to ensure a strong Congo and so bring pressure upon the remaining European strongholds in Angola, Rhodesia, and South Africa. I suspect, as a matter of fact, that the Europeans had a better understanding and appreciation of Ghana's stand than the Americans, who were utterly obsessed with their fear of Communism. (Now the reverse is the case; the United States has put its finger on the root causes of the Congo's difficulties and has made ceaseless efforts to find constructive solutions.) But we did not give up when Lumumba was murdered. We gave every support to the cause of constitutional legality by recognizing Antoine Gizenga as the lawful heir of Lumumba until the Parliament of the Congo reconvened to approve a new central government and a new Prime Minister, and our stand has, I am sure, played a part in the restoration of legality to the Congo. I may say, too, that I was one of the first to suggest, prophetically, that Cyrile Adoula, a trade-unionist and independent politician, could be elected Prime Minister and salvage the situation; soon thereafter, thanks to the full support given him by the Lumumbists (the Nationalist Front), Adoula was indeed elected Prime Minister by the Congolese Parliament. In the end, therefore, it was the Casablanca Group of African states—Algeria, Ghana, Guinea, Mali, Morocco, and the United Arab Republic—that was vindicated, not those who maintained that the chief of state alone had the power to make and break prime ministers in the Congo.

The Congo crisis not only provided a severe test of African solidarity, but nearly broke it in two. In spite of the crisis, how-

ever, the African Personality seems to have survived; if it has
not gained strength, it has certainly stood its ground. That is indeed important, for the great struggle for world supremacy between two major ideologies is sure to continue; as long as it continues, Africa, like it or not, is certain to be involved, since
neither of the two great powers will be willing to stand aside.
Africa must continue to remain strong—morally strong, at least
—so that it may take a positively independent approach to the
problems of the world. And if Africa asserts herself positively and
objectively, is it unreasonable to expect that other nations and
continents will eventually follow suit? It is my conviction, at
least, that Africa can emerge as a vital and steadying influence,
a constant in a changing world, and, by example, make it incum-
bent upon both East and West to come to grips with the realities
of the African situation. At the moment, the determination of
Africa to rid itself of colonialism seems to place the continent in
opposition to the West; but such a determination, which has
been openly supported by the Soviet bloc, need not be interpreted to mean that Africa is therefore anti-Western or pro-
Eastern. It is the colonial powers of Western Europe, after all,
that still retain control in Africa, and it is migrants from Western
Europe who still make up the dominant white population in
Africa; after Africa's long and exhausting experience under colonial control, it is not at all unnatural that the pendulum should
swing toward the total rejection of the colonial powers and all
their works. Even now, as freedom and independence sweep
through Africa, there are still many African territories, including
the Congo, Northern and Southern Rhodesia, Mozambique,
South-West Africa, and South Africa, that are being cruelly ex-
ploited by colonial and white oppression. The situation in these
parts of Africa is so terrible, so inhuman that ordinary Europeans
and Americans would recoil in horror if they learned the truth of
what is being perpetrated against African men and women,
against ordinary people like themselves, who have the same

hopes, fears, desires, and needs. The awful truth is that the Europeans in Africa have always arrogated to themselves superior powers, and they will, I fear, go to any lengths to maintain their minority power over the African majority.

What is, however, so hopeful about Africa's determination to rid the continent of colonial rule, racial discrimination, and white supremacy is that it is not imbued with a desire for vengeance. If it were, the white man would have found it impossible to remain in Africa until now, and many independent African states would not have continued, as they obviously have, to maintain friendly links with Europe and the Europeans. The point is, of course, that the Africans wish to liquidate not the Europeans themselves but the system of colonialism and racial oppression they introduced into Africa, and when that is fully accomplished, Africa will not only be completely free but much more able than perhaps she is at present to take an impartial, objective attitude toward the West. Indeed, she must if she is to accomplish her aims, and the years that lie immediately ahead are certainly crucial ones. It is paradoxical, in fact, that the re-emergence of Africa should be occurring at the very moment that the world, although ideologically divided between East and West, is striving for unity. For that reason alone, Africa cannot and will not remain isolated, and it is important that she does not, that she continues to assert the African Personality.

My final reason for saying that the African Personality must continue to be asserted is that the voice of Africa has yet to be heard fully. The voice of Africa, uttered through her sons and daughters, must, I am convinced, continue to draw attention to the injustices and the oppression suffered over the centuries by the African peoples. There are those, of course, who tell us that they have already heard enough, but generally they are the very ones who do not wish the balance to be redressed, the past to be expurgated, the future to be different. They do not, in short, wish Africa to assume its rightful place in the assembly of nations. But

I submit that the tale is not yet fully told, the balance has yet to be struck. Although the main outlines of the situation have been published, a psychological revolution is still needed before Africans and their former oppressors can come to a full understanding of the new era that is dawning. The fact that Africa was oppressed and has now recovered her freedom must sink deeply into the consciousness of the world before we can pass on to the next phase of world history. Then, and only then, can we echo the words uttered, as if in a moment of discovery, by the late HIH Prince Sahle Selassie of Ethiopia at the Accra Conference: "Africa has spoken!"